THE
RISING
LEADER
Handbook

THE
RISING
LEADER
Handbook

TURNING HIGH ACHIEVERS
INTO EFFECTIVE LEADERS

MARK J. SILVERMAN

Endorsements

"Silverman's book is the most thorough, transformative, and compelling book on leadership I have ever read."

~ **Steve Chandler,** author, *Time Warrior*

"In today's world there is a poverty of imagination — people simply do not know what is possible for them. In The Rising Leader Handbook, Mark J. Silverman raises your self-belief and, through detailed examples, models, and worksheets, turns your success as a leader from a possibility to a certainty."

~ **James Whittaker,** (3x bestselling author, Success Magazine speaker, and leading authority on how to Win the Day®)

"We still live in a world where so many people identify leadership by role or title. In The Rising Leader Handbook, Mark J. Silverman challenges us to understand that leadership is a transformational journey where we continuously learn and develop our own art of leadership. Mark reminds us that it is possible for each of us to lead and be our best in every situation we face."

~ **Geoffrey Roche,** Director of Workforce Development at Siemens Healthineers

"I highly recommend The Rising Leader Handbook by Mark J. Silverman. I worked with Mark at two different companies and he distinguished himself in short order both times. It's been inspiring to watch him develop into a leadership voice using some of the same things that made him such a successful seller."

~ **Kevin Haverty,** Vice Chair Global Public Sector ServiceNow

"Inspirational and practical wisdom to teach you how to be the leader you aspire to be."

~ **Alisa Cohn,** author *From Start-up to Grown-up*

"... an essential read for every rising leader. Having worked with Mark for a number of years, I trust his approach will show very real and very tangible results — not only making you more effective but also happier."

~ **Stuart Lammin,** CEO RNHB

"Mark Silverman is the real deal. A powerful practitioner who leads by example and has committed his life to doing the hard and essential inner work that makes the world a better place. In his new book, he brings the lessons every leader needs for transformational impact."

~ **Teo Alfero,** founder Wolf Connection sanctuary and author, *The Wolf Connection*

"The Rising Leader Handbook is full of actionable tools and practical insights that will help any leader, at any stage, and in any industry raise (and sustain) their game!"

~ **Alan Stein Jr.,** author, *Sustain Your Game*

"The Rising Leader Handbook is a rare combination of many useful insights on multiple aspects of leadership ... and practical ways to implement them. This same approach is why Mark has become such a successful, sought-after, executive coach."

~ **Tom Mendoza,** former President/Vice Chair NetApp

"Mark J. Silverman has written an essential guide for Leading Up, Leading Across, Leading the Team and Leading Oneself, all with heart and impact."

~ **Mark C. Crowley,** author, *Lead From The Heart*

"Mark J. Silverman's The Rising Leader Handbook brilliantly guides top performers to lead with impact. It's a roadmap to excellence in leadership, combining effective strategy with practical action steps. A must-read for anyone aspiring to lead with impact and integrity."

~ **Rich Litvin,** founder of 4PC and coauthor,
The Prosperous Coach

"Over the years, I've admired Mark's genuine courage and leadership. He's transformed his life and career because he refused to settle for soul-crushing personal and professional situations. In an industry saturated with leadership-clones and business-book-blowhards, Mark leads by example with brains, guts, and heart."

~ **Tripp Lanier,** professional coach and author,
This Book Will Make You Dangerous

"Unlike most of my leadership books collecting dust on my shelves, The Rising Leader Handbook sits dog-eared and underlined on my desk. Mark J. Silverman does a masterful job of synthesizing critically important leadership concepts and behaviors into easily implementable, practical and tactical advice that all leaders – new and experienced -- can benefit from. If you are striving to develop and hone your leadership skills, you need to read this book.

~ **Matt Abrahams,** Stanford GSB Strategic Communication
Lecturer, author, *Think Faster Talk Smarter,*
and Think Fast Talk Smart The Podcast host.

"Drawing from over six years of working with Mark, I can attest to the depth of insight and practical wisdom he brings to the table. In The Rising Leader Handbook, Mark distills his extensive experience and profound understanding of leadership into actionable strategies that empower individuals to ascend to their fullest potential. Whether you're a seasoned executive, an aspiring entrepreneur, or simply someone eager to enhance their leadership skills, this book offers invaluable guidance to navigate the complexities of today's dynamic world.

~ **Sean McDermott,** CEO Windward Consulting

"Mark's years of experience as an executive coach shine through in this book. Read this book full of proven tools and strategies if you want to accelerate your career or grow the high performers on your team."

~ **Helen Appleby,** author
The Unwritten Rules of Women's Leadership

"The Rising Leader Handbook articulates the foundational principles of leadership in an accessible way that will resonate with any leader, regardless of their tenure."

~ **John Sapone,** Senior Vice President of Sales Snowflake

"Move over Peter Drucker, we have a new modern management thought leader in town. I spent twenty-six years in the corporate world, working my way up to the C-suite at Harley-Davidson. Silverman crystallized so many insights and ideas I wish I would've understood much earlier on that journey — not the least of which about responsibility, empathy, and self. This is a must-have manual for leaders who want more impact and fulfillment, less frustration and burnout."

~ **Shelley Paxton,** current Chief Soul Officer/speaker/author,
Soulbbatical and former Chief Marketing Officer
of Harley-Davidson

"I have known Mark for over twenty years and have personally witnessed both his career and personal evolution. What I admire about Mark and this book is that he takes you on a journey with him: he has lived and experienced everything that you are reading and used all his learnings to become the best version of himself. You are the beneficiary of all his deep work."

~**Beth Perlman,** Managing Director, Chief Information
Officer Advisor, Think Consulting

"With over seventeen years of coaching high-level professionals, I enthusiastically recommend Silverman's book as an indispensable guide for mastering the art of communication. Brimming with unparalleled insights, diverse perspectives, and a treasure trove of valuable resources, this book stands out for its transformative advice. A must-read for anyone serious about advancing their career, honing communication skills, and achieving excellence."

~ **Karen Davis,** executive coach and coauthor of
How to Get the Most Out of Coaching,
A Client's Guide for Optimizing the Coaching Experience

"Mark's honest and heartfelt approach not only equips leaders to triumph in business, but also achieve personal happiness and fulfillment. The innovative leadership skills in The Rising Leader Handbook will transform and uplevel your own success and self-worth, while generating ripple effects that boost morale and productivity across your organization."

~ **Sarah Kate Ellis,** GLAAD President and CEO,
TIME100 Honoree

"The Rising Leader Handbook is a treasure trove of practical wisdom, perfectly tailored for real-world application. This isn't just a book about leading in the office; it's a guide for leadership in all walks of life. Silverman's focus on transforming situations and taking ownership across diverse scenarios is deeply empowering. His book offers tools to not just survive, but thrive. For anyone seeking to leave a real mark in leadership, this handbook is a must read!"

~ **Laurie Arron,** author *Who Has Your Back?*

"Mark J. Silverman distinguishes himself among his contemporaries. He emulates the commitment to self-reflection and responsibility that he advocates in a very human way for his clients, listeners and readers. His unique ability to embody what a rising leader needs to be is his greatest gift to all of us."

~ **Dr. Jeff Spencer,** champion builder, speaker and author

In loving memory of Barry Silverman.
Brother, son, uncle, friend—
without you, none of this would be possible.

And to my family.
John, thank you for the amazing dinners and saying,
"Go to your office and write."

Zack and Jake (Yakkov), nothing creates a leader like fatherhood.
You inspire me.

TABLE OF CONTENTS

Leading Your Team

SUCCESS THROUGH OTHERS

Leading You

BEING YOUR BEST IN ALL SITUATIONS

Introduction

SKYDIVING IN THE OFFICE — WORK DOESN'T HAVE TO BE "SOUL-CRUSHING"

I was walking my dogs yesterday listening to the audio version of *The Lion Trackers Guide to Life* by Boyd Varty. He grew up on a game preserve in South Africa where he learned how to track animals in the bush from the local experts. Varty applies the wisdom and skills honed from his experiences to his writing, coaching, and workshops. It is an inspiring and insightful perspective on personal development.

In the book, Varty describes people coming to his workshops as, "half dead from soul-crushing corporate jobs." His impression isn't wrong, and it's one shared by many in the self-help space. A lot of us *are* walking around less than thrilled with life, feeling like being in an office is death, and Varty offers the contrasting glimpse of how lion tracking is life. I found myself easily agreeing. Yet it occurred to me that my work was showing me another facet of this.

Corporate jobs could crush your spirit while skydiving or surfing bring you alive. Danger forces us to be present ... and being present is being in touch with life.

I just got back from scuba diving with sharks. It was exhilarating.

While there is a ton of truth in the contrast between working in corporate life and something like scuba diving, this is also a mind trap. Most of us did not grow up on a game preserve, near a great surf spot, or with a $3000 mountain bike to race down ski slopes with. I grew up on Long Island, and our ski slope was Bald Hill.

To survive, most of us need to get a job or start a business. We work for promotions. If you live in the United States, you need health insurance through an employer, or your kids won't see adulthood. Most of us will live within the boundaries of what Boyd Varty might consider mundane.

My perspective has a slight adaptation. I believe in the immediacy and danger of life in every moment. There are opportunities to feel alive and on a knife's edge right here, right now.

- Take a job you aren't qualified for
- Step on a stage in front of 6 or 6000 people and share your perspective
- Speak truth to power
- Disagree with a room full of colleagues
- Be vulnerable with your significant other
- Give an employee constructive, honest feedback
- Sing karaoke
- Start a business
- Make art
- Put down your phone, take a deep breath, and experience whatever is here and now

I swear. Your nerve endings will tingle like you are standing at the door of a plane waiting to skydive when you set a difficult boundary or ask for a date.

LIFE IS NOW, WHEREVER YOU ARE.

Life is only soul-crushing if you decide it is. You may be in a job you don't like. You may desire something more impactful. I did. I changed careers.

I became an executive coach when I was 50, risking my finances and all I had built, because I wanted to make a difference. I had witnessed the unspoken agreement we all were making to be in the 1%. I saw the broken marriages, poor health, addiction, and even death from the stress of our soul-crushing relationship with success.

I don't disagree with Boyd Varty, I just know we can make the shift without having to do extreme, dangerous things or risking what we care about.

To that end, this "leadership book" is about living life to the fullest, creating robust relationships, having powerful impact, and savoring a satisfying life every day.

Your version of skydiving is showing up your best for those who count on you.

Your lion tracking will be living your values every day.

Your Banzai Pipeline will be realizing your full potential.

"WHAT GOT YOU HERE WON'T GET YOU WHERE YOU WANT TO GO."

You know it. You've been successful, just the way you are, for a long time, probably since high school. You've out-worked, relied on your subject matter expertise, charm, niceness, or your bull-in-a-china-shop way of doing things.

What got you here has been pretty good so far. And ... it's holding you back.

- Your inability to let go of the details—*Holding you back!*
- Your not paying attention to the details—*Holding you back!*
- Your cutthroat way of dealing with the other team leads—*Holding you back!*
- Your inability to hold people accountable—*Holding you back!*

- Your affability—*Holding you back!*
- Your not speaking up to the boss, your speaking up way too much, your micromanaging, your burning the candle at both ends, your lack of self-confidence, your know-it-all-ness, your inability to give credit, and your need for recognition—*All, holding you back.*

If the things that got you where you are no longer serve you, now what?

There are three questions to ask yourself …

1– What do I need to leave behind?

2– Where do I need to level up?

3– Who do I need to be?

It's daunting. Too many people can't even ask the questions above, much less let go of what has worked for so long as part of the answer. You know these people. You've worked for them, those folks who just don't mature into their new role or level of responsibility. You work around them. You get things done *in spite of them.*

You *don't* want to be them.

The following are a couple of conversations I have had with CEOs about their "high achievers."

"Mark, John is a rock star. He has more industry and institutional knowledge than my entire leadership team. He has great ideas and almost always knows the right path. But getting him to speak up is almost impossible. I want him to head up a new acquisition next year, but I can't if he doesn't speak up in leadership meetings."

"Mark, I want Sherri to be our next CFO as the current one transitions out. She knows the business inside and out, has our back on everything, but works herself into a stressed state. She's

a lovely person, but snaps at her people and the others on the leadership team. I can't get her to let go of some of the day-to-day to focus on the strategic initiatives we need for this next phase of growth."

Basically, they are asking for their "high achiever" to become more of an "effective leader." John and Sherri are recognized for "what got them here," and are now being asked to acquire new skills to get to the next level.

"There are studies from very legitimate organizations that net out the failure rate of managers, whether you're talking about brand new managers all the way up to the C suite. The 18-month failure rate is around 60%. It's worse than a coin flip, that you will still be allowed to lead that team 18 months from now.

Then there's another stat, which is, most people leave their jobs because they dislike their manager. Yet, we know that in order to drive societal improvements, to give employment to people, we achieve more together than apart. When we put people together, we need leaders."

David Kline, co-founder MGMT Accelerator
The Rising Leader Podcast episode 28:
"Accelerating Leadership"
https://bit.ly/47q4cCa

The good news is that "leadership is a learned skill," as my friend Alisa Cohn says in her book, *From Start Up to Grown Up, Grow Your Leadership to Grow Your Business*. Alisa shares story after story of entrepreneurs and founders who start businesses without the experience they need at the outset, and how she guides them through the different stages of growing their business. Like you, they learn on the job.

"When I spoke to Suzy [Batiz, founder of Poo-Pourri and one of the eighty richest self-made women in the US according to Forbes] about imposter syndrome, she told me, "I don't have imposter syndrome. I AM an imposter! I have never run a company this size before. We're all doing things for the first time and figuring it out." Give yourself a break and embrace the journey."

When I read Alisa Cohn's book, I couldn't help but see the parallel challenges of running a fast-growing company and moving up the ladder in an organization.

Listen to my discussion with Alisa Cohn on *Mastering Overwhelm* episode 8 (https://bit.ly/40M3Occ).

You can (and will) expand your range to include the traits and behaviors you need to get where you want to go.

Let's get started.

EFFECTIVE LEADERSHIP STARTS WITH YOU

Up-leveling is an internal job first, and a skills-sharpening job second.

For every challenge you face, conversation you need to have, and outcome you want to influence, we will absolutely discuss tools and strategies. Yet, before we play whac-a-mole with behaviors, we will start with internal shifts.

"I realized I needed to change, to grow as a leader in those moments when I would blow people out of the water, and make them feel like shit, even when I had good intentions. Because of the reactive and the emotional way that I went about it, it changed my dynamic with that person or with that entire group of people. I was ultra-sensitive to how it was affecting my relationships in my business and the direction that I wanted to go. So, each step of the way, I've read hundreds of books, mostly on leadership and communication. I never wanted to make people feel like that again, ever in my life. I would prefer that I can handle this better next time, stay regulated, stay composed, and be thoughtful with the way that I handle these situations."

Jefferson K. Rogers, CEO JKR Windows
The Rising Leader Podcast episode 11:
"Intuition, Health, and Leadership"
https://bit.ly/3sGMitj

The first shift: when things don't go your way, it's easy to blame.

Instead of blaming ... when faced with a situation that needs a new or different response, ask yourself:

- What part have I played in creating this situation?
- Who am I being?
- What am I believing?
- How am I speaking?
- What am I willing (and not willing) to do?
- What am I willing to give up?
- What am I willing to embrace?

Don't worry, as we work through the four parts of the books, I will give you enough practice that the above questions and asking them of yourself will become second nature.

ATTITUDE ADJUSTMENT

Unflinching self-reflection and taking 100% responsibility for how you are showing up will make all the difference.

Leaders take 100% responsibility for themselves, their team, and the circumstances they find themselves in, whether or not it is their fault.

You may balk at this assertion. That's okay.

Resistance and uncomfortable feelings are a feature, not a bug when leveling up.

Every expansion comes with resistance.

You will be moving out of your comfort zone and old ways of being. Your ego may chafe when I ask you to say, "I got this," to something that wasn't even your fault, rather than blame.

Answering the questions above for yourself puts you in the driver's seat. You retain your power. It will help you understand yourself in any given situation and give you the direction you need to challenge yourself.

Leaders grow from the challenge.

"It is not the critic who counts; not the man who points out how the strong man stumbles, or where the doer of deeds could have done them better. The credit belongs to the man who is actually in the arena, whose face is marred by dust and sweat and blood; who strives valiantly; who errs, who comes short again and again, because there is no effort without error and shortcoming; but who does actually strive to do the deeds; who knows great enthusiasms, the great devotions; who spends himself in a worthy cause; who at the best knows in the end the triumph of high achievement, and who at the worst, if he fails, at least fails while daring greatly, so that his place shall never be with those cold and timid souls who neither know victory nor defeat."

~ Theodore Roosevelt

HOW THIS BOOK IS STRUCTURED

The book is written in four sections:

Leading Up – Becoming a Trusted Advisor

Leading Across – Leading on a Team of Peers

Leading Your Team – Success Through Others

Leading You – Being Your Best In All Situations

Leading You is last intentionally. (I know, it's a little strange, but it works.)

We will use interactions with your boss, peers, and team as a mirror for the internal shifts and actions you need to take in your journey to becoming more effective. Think of it as "on the job training." By the time we get to Leading You, you will have done much of the work in real world situations. What will be left is some integration and a focus on topics like: well-being, relationships, and fun. You have got to have fun, or why work so hard?

You can also go directly to the section that applies to your challenge today.

At work and at home, the ability to take an active role in creating the quality and direction of your life leads to greater levels of fulfillment and satisfaction. It is the lack of these two things people cite when they say they are "stuck in soul-crushing jobs and lives."

This book is not about getting a soul-crushing job to suck less.

It is about thriving in every situation. And taking the steps to change a situation you do not like.

Leadership is not just about the job, the team, or getting results.

Whether in a group of people working a challenging problem, raising children, or in your romantic relationship, leadership is about taking ownership of whatever hand you are dealt, playing it well, and recreating it every day.

Living a default life is hard. Creating the career, life, and relationships you want is also hard, but with leadership, it's possible.

CHOOSE YOUR HARD.

A NOTE ABOUT WHAT I ADMIRE IN A LEADER

Tom Mendoza has been the quintessential example of the leader I strive to be, and a mentor for over 20 years. The very first time I encountered him, I marveled at how he treated every person in a crowded room whether they were visibly powerful or reserved. He would walk up to someone standing alone and introduce himself and then introduce them to others. That was the leader I wanted to be.

After leaving NetApp, I wrote a list for myself, The Top Ten Things I Learned from Tom Mendoza:

1. Never speak badly about anyone.

2. Look for the people in a room that seem uncomfortable and be welcoming. Bring them in.

3. Be passionate about what you do…if you are not, find your passion and if you cannot find it, find something different you can be passionate about.

4. Customers are lifelong relationships. Your job is their success first and foremost.

5. Competitive means doing your absolute best, improving and learning as you go. Gracious when you lose, Gracious when you win.

6. You are the culture of an organization. It starts with you.

7. Lead by example.

8. Catch someone doing something right…And tell them and everyone.

9. The CEO, the People in Shipping, Admin or cleaning the bathrooms all contribute to our success. Treat everyone with the same respect.

10. Find the fun in a very tough job.

Leading Up

BECOMING A TRUSTED ADVISOR

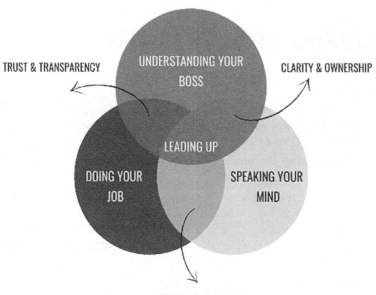

Chapter 1

BECOMING A TRUSTED ADVISOR

"Firstly, I want my trusted advisors to have the company's interest at heart. I want people who will state their opinion. We want candor in the executive team meeting. If the door closes we assume we are on the same page. If you didn't speak don't come back later.

By the way it was true of almost all employees. We had a culture of candor."

Tom Mendoza former President/Vice Chair NetApp
The Rising Leader Podcast episode 30:
"People-Centered Leadership"
https://bit.ly/3GBX3Rb

Our goal is to have maximum and immediate impact.

I most often get hired directly by CEOs. They have a very talented high achiever on their leadership team and they want more for them and from them. If I can shift one or two things that make our high achiever a more effective leader in the eyes of the CEO, we are off to a fast start.

The scenario usually goes as follows:

A few weeks after I start with a client, I typically get a call from the CEO who hired me, and they say, "What did you do to Charlie? He's a different person."

Charlie and I worked on how he shows up in this situation and he was able to make the change once he understood the impact of his behavior and why he was acting in this manner.

We do this work in the trenches, like I did with Charlie, in real time, and get tangible results quickly. We had an objective, Charlie had incentive, we made visible progress, fast.

I want your up-levelling to be noticed as fast as possible, like Charlie's, so we start with the relationship with *your boss*.

To influence and support those who are in higher positions in the organization, your goal needs to be to create strong relationships, gain trust, promote change, and obtain support for your ideas or initiatives. Influence starts with listening and understanding.

Let's start with information gathering.

You need to get to know who you work for.

"Every opportunity I ever got was because someone wanted to help me. I am now three times the beneficiary of people who really decided to help me when I wasn't smart enough to ask for their help. And yet, they were still motivated. What is it about me? Why would people invest in me as opposed to just playing golf or helping the person next to me? You'd have to ask them in some ways, but I think there are a number of things that come out of it.

It's ... the obligation it imposes upon me to help others, give them the kind of assistance that I've been the beneficiary of throughout my entire career. And I realized the answer to the question, "How does a skinny black kid from an island of 35,000 people become the global CIO of the world's largest professional services firm?"

When I'm on your team, I'm on your team, I'll argue with you all, I'll give you my point of view. I'm not going to backstab you or angle for your job.

Second, I understand that part of my job is to get it right. I grew up playing cricket, baseball is the equivalent, you only get a certain number of at bats. You got to take some swings. If you don't swing at the ball, you're not going to accomplish anything. If you played safe, you're not going to accomplish anything. If you swing at everything, you're going to be out all the time. You get a certain number of at bats, and you get to get a great batting average. You got to swing at some balls, and you got to hit the right percentage of them. You're responsible for that. And you're responsible for making that happen.

I figured out that I really cared about the team. I really cared about people. I got energy from talking to a bright team member in my office, listening to what they said and really caring about how they felt, what they wanted to do, their aspirations, their lives, even if they were saving money in a 401K. I cared. And I learned that about myself because I'm actually an introvert. So as an introvert, sometimes you think, that that's not you. And I actually figured out, yeah, I'm an introvert, but I care about people."

Larry Quinlan, former Global CIO of Deloitte
The Rising Leader Podcast episode 34:
"Leadership, Humility and Success"
https://bit.ly/3slCyie

UNDERSTANDING THE BOSS

ATTITUDE ADJUSTMENT

Making the relationship with your boss work is your job, regardless of whether they are the feature personality for *Leadership Magazine* or a candidate for anger management class.

I have thrived working for more than a few amazing bosses.

I have quit jobs I loved because of a bad boss.

I have outlasted bad bosses only to be surprised by a great one.

I have gotten along with, and thrived where the boss was a challenge for most people but I had cracked the code.

IT'S NOT ABOUT YOUR BOSS.

It's about how you show up with whoever your boss is. Mastering the art of Leading Up will give you the greatest chance at the best relationship with whatever kind of boss you have.

> **"** The quality of your working relationships determines your success and your happiness. Stop leaving it to chance and start building the best possible relationships. Not every relationship is going to be fantastic, but every one could be better."
>
> **~ Michael Bungay Stanier,**
> How to Work with Almost Anyone

Every relationship is a 200% endeavor—both parties are 100% responsible for their side of the street. The challenge for you is that you cannot control your boss' side of the street, which means you have to be outstanding at street maintenance.

New Client: *"But Mark, he has a bad temper, he jumps from project to project with the same urgency, undermines me with my team, drinks all day, smells bad ..."*

It's often one of the first things I hear at the beginning of a coaching agreement.

Mark: *"I totally understand. You are right, he shouldn't be that way. If I were coaching your boss, I would confront him with all the litter on his side of the street. I would make sure he understood that it is 100% his responsibility to create the relationship with you. I am not coaching your boss today."*

Client: *"But, shouldn't he change?"*

Mark: *"Of course, but that is out of our control."*

How often have you tried to change someone? How'd that work out for you?

Most bosses come out on the net positive side of the scale, and it's human to focus on the rough edges you are working with.

What I'd like to eradicate early is the "victim" mindset and also the language that is easy to fall prey to. Remember, 100% responsibility.

"When you argue with reality, you only lose 100% of the time."

~ Byron Katie

You can always quit, call HR and complain, or argue all day. Or you can adjust and play the hand you are dealt … well.

I'm not saying you can't set healthy boundaries. Boundaries and clear communication are very different from trying to change someone. They are tools for taking 100% responsibility *for your side of the street*. I will never support you to be a doormat.

Of course, if you are dealing with abuse or legal/integrity issues, you should probably quit. I have quit on out-of-control bosses, and it is liberating.

But please remember, you are never a victim. You have options.

I want you to thrive with a great boss.

Recreate a relationship with a difficult boss.

Be the master of your own destiny, no matter your boss.

HOW WELL DO YOU KNOW YOUR BOSS?

"My ROTC Captain taught us how to be a dynamic subordinate. He went out of his way to say, "I'm not talking about how to kiss your boss's ass, I'm talking about being a great subordinate." And he explained to us the dynamic of what it's like to be a boss. You're under pressure, there's a lot of things coming at you. And sometimes, especially when you're early in career, you don't really have an appreciation for that. So, you're maybe passing in something late or incomplete etc., and making their job harder. Jack Welch is the former CEO of GE, his advice for early career people was make your boss' job easier. Try to be the person who helps your boss solve some problems. That, in and of itself, will get you to the top of the stack rank if you're doing everything else well."

Kevin Haverty, Senior Advisor to the CEO of ServiceNow
The Rising Leader Podcast episode 13:
"Rising from Super Sales Rep to Effective Leader"
https://bit.ly/3MPXafp

You are a tennis player. Tomorrow is your center court debut at Wimbledon. Your opponent is the #1 seed. Would you step on that hallowed grass without doing your homework? Would you show up in front of millions of people, about to fulfill the dreams you had since you were 5 years old, that you sweated for when you were taken out of school to practice eight hours a day, forfeiting a normal childhood for, without studying every aspect of the other players' game?

No. You'd know their strengths, weaknesses, and mindset. You would know when they go to the net and when they drop back. You would try to get into their head, wouldn't you?

So, why would you do anything less with your boss?

The good news is you don't need to attend a special camp for a decade and sacrifice your childhood to master the game. Fifteen minutes of reflection, and the willingness to ask the right questions, listen, and observe will do. Then, with a little effort to keep what you learn top of mind, you are prepared for center court.

I promise, it will pay dividends.

BUILDING OUR BOSS EMPATHY MAP

"Curiosity is a means to an end of building relationship that works for everybody involved. We prefer to be in relationship with people, they prefer to be in relationship with us. People are kind of the messy, complex, brilliant human being that they are. When you can be present with them, see them for all of that, and connect to them on a really human level it works better."

Michael Bungay Stanier, author of *How to Work with (Almost) Anyone*,
The Coaching Habit and various other wonderful titles
The Rising Leader Podcast episode 21:
"Curiosity-Based Leadership"
https://bit.ly/3RS9uO8

You will be tempted to do these exercises in your head—don't.

You will retain more and see things differently when they are in black and white on the page.

ROLES AND RESPONSIBILITIES

- What is their actual job description?
- What are their official roles and responsibilities?
- What are their unofficial roles and responsibilities?
- What does success look like for them? How are they rewarded?
- What does failure look like for them? How does it affect their position or compensation?

FEARS AND TRIGGERS

- What sets them off?
- When do they get anxious? When do they relax?
- How do they prefer their communication?
- What frustrates them?
- What's behind what they constantly ask for?

VALUES

- How do they present themselves? Listen to what they "say" they value, even if they themselves do not live up to the standard.
- What do they care about professionally? Personally?
- What/who do they judge harshly?

ULTIMATE GOAL

- What are they trying to accomplish?
- How are they measured?
- What does success look like for them?
- What is the why behind all of it? (Look beyond the obvious.)

EMPATHY IS THE SECRET TO BUILDING A RELATIONSHIP WITH ANYONE, INCLUDING YOUR BOSS.

Let's Reflect

After spending time in your boss' shoes:

- knowing a portion of their roles and responsibilities, how has your perspective shifted?
- knowing their fears and triggers, when is your boss calm and relaxed?
- What can YOU do to help your boss feel calmer and more relaxed? Master this skill and you will be invaluable.

- knowing what they value in life and in their people, how can you demonstrate more of these values, or shine a light on where you share them?

- knowing their Ultimate Goal, how can you align yourself with that goal?

When you get to know your boss as a human with talents and faults, challenges, and responsibilities, it softens harsh judgments, and helps you gain empathy. With your newfound understanding, you can really become that trusted advisor.

THE CLARITY CONVERSATION

Set a meeting with your boss for the expressed reason to become a better partner in helping them reach their objectives. Be upfront and honest.

- "I am trying to understand you better so I can be more effective in our communication."

- "What do you need from me that I may not be doing, that would be helpful?"

- "My official job, and how I am measured is X. Y falls on my plate regularly, how would you like me to prioritize this?"

Your boss is going to feel great knowing you want to do your part in creating an outstanding working relationship. They will also be open to your needs. It is the perfect time to have that conversation as well. Be specific and brief.

- "I understand instructions best this way."

- "I get nervous when I think I don't understand fully, would you please give me extra time for questions so I can be clear when we finish a meeting?"

- "My daughter has dance recitals on Thursday evenings. Unless there is an emergency, I will be with her."

ATTITUDE ADJUSTMENT:

Clarity is your responsibility.

We just spent some time playing "boss bingo." You are looking at your card and there are some gaps in understanding. It may be in communication style, unofficial responsibilities, side goals, etc.

It's time to ask.

SIX BOSS PERSONALITIES

Many companies have personality assessments as part of their regular operating principles. If yours does, see if you can get a copy of your boss'. If you have one of your own, share with each other the strengths and challenges uncovered. You will be surprised by the effectiveness of this exercise in vulnerability.

Personality assessments like to put us in a box of traits and behaviors. I have done the same here by generalizing a few. With each "type," I offer solutions my clients have found effective. Remember, you or your boss are not a "type", we just need a frame of reference for our discussion.

ARE THEY AN IDEA MACHINE?

Most visionaries come up with project after project, and they can't help it. They got where they are because they live in "what's possible." They live to create and are impatient with implementation.

In their great book, *Rocket Fuel*, Gino Wickman and Mark C. Winters separate folks into Visionaries (idea machines) and Integrators (those who get it done). Their observations?

There are seven visionaries to every one integrator. A visionary without an integrator is usually broke. It is the integrator's job to focus (not stifle) the visionary on what can actually be done.

You may also be a natural visionary yourself, but if you are a trusted advisor, your role will lean towards integrator.

Back to considering your boss.

ARE THEY A MICROMANAGER?

Do they need to be in every meeting, sign every paper and have you report back every step of the way? A Micromanager has issues with trust and control.

ARE THEY IN THE WEEDS?

Do they too actively participate in what you and the team are working at? If so, they are different than the micromanager because they want to be your friend. They want to lead as peers, be in the trenches. They often feel useless in their new position, so they lean on old familiar tasks. They work hard, which is admirable, but nobody is steering the ship.

ARE THEY A CREDIT HOG?

Do they take too much credit for the team's work? Do they use the word I when it's really you, or we? Do people on the team feel resentment because they aren't recognized for their hard work? You may have a Credit Hog on your hands.

ARE THEY A RAGE-A-HOLIC?

Does your boss react with rage? Are they great much of the time, but you never know when the other shoe will drop? The Rage-a-Holic can't handle their own fear and overwhelm, so they go on the offensive wiping out any goodwill they have built with the team.

ARE THEY TOXIC?

They may be a toxic boss or just plain awful. Awful can come in many flavors—dishonest, manipulative, inappropriate, or abusive. These bosses are toxic. There are just some things that are unacceptable, and action needs to be taken.

Have you identified some of your boss' characteristics? Remember, nobody fits perfectly in a box. Most of us can be a combination of "types" in different situations or frames of mind. Let's talk about the best ways to handle some of the behaviors that may be difficult to deal with.

THE IDEA MACHINE

- Set clear boundaries. They often won't know how hard they are pushing the team. They come from enthusiasm and can be oblivious to the impact of it.

- Have regular "agreements" conversations. You must be on the same page, document, and revisit. They will forget what they agreed to. Keep them on track.

- Help them prioritize by giving them information on timelines, resources, and obstacles.

- Never say, "No." Say, "We could do that, and this will be the impact…"

THE MICROMANAGER

- Speak to their fear – lack of control.
- Over-communicate.
- Over-communicate.
- Over-communicate.

THE IN THE WEEDS LEADER

- Set aside your ego and allow them to be involved.
- Set boundaries when they affect your work quality or productivity.
- Assure them you "have this."
- Their coach or superior is the one to help change their behavior.

THE CREDIT HOG

- Document your work.
- Pick your battles. If it is important to you, set the boundary outside the meeting.
- Know that people *know* who is really doing the work.

THE RAGE-A-HOLIC

- Set strong and immediate boundaries when lines are crossed.
- Don't take it personally—it is their fear, not your performance. If you can do that, you will be able to act with more clarity.
- What is the message behind the rage? What do they fear? What do they need? It's often a form of safety or control.
- Do they need to feel safe or in control?
- Anger is a secondary emotion covering fear or sadness.
- Is this an occasional outburst or the norm? If it is the norm…

THE TOXIC BOSS

- Are you safe?
- Is it worth the fight?
- Get help.
- Be willing to walk.

No job is worth feeling (or being) unsafe or miserable. If you have a toxic boss, and cannot find resolution through the support system of the organization, it's time to leave.

Life is short, don't waste it on them.

Now that you understand your boss a little better …write down at least three things you can do to manage yourself, them, and your relationship better. I have a scenario for you.

John's boss Katie is awesome. She is dynamic, creative, driven, and charismatic. Everyone loves Katie. The problem is she can be quite harsh when she's stressed. It isn't often but she lashes out and it can take days for the object of her ire to recover. It is a real problem for the company, and she is working on getting better. Slowly.

John told me he can barely focus for days after a verbal altercation. He turns it on himself and avoids her until he can find his footing. The problem is, he's Katie's trusted advisor.

I gave him some perspective. "Anger is a secondary emotion, in Katie's case, it's hiding fear. Fear feels weak so she uses anger to feel more powerful and in control. If you could stay in the conversation, know it's not you, and ask questions to find out what she needs to address her fear, you'll find she calms down quickly."

John, "that makes sense. I can try that."

"Also know, if someone is angry with you at about a 3 or 4 level, it could be about the thing. If they come at you at a 5 or above, it's no longer the thing. It's overwhelm, fear, or childhood trauma. It is something other than what you are talking about. In fact, you are no longer there and Katie (all of us) is raging at a ghost. So again, don't take it on."

We talked more about how he handles conflict and how Katie triggers his childhood wounds. We decided that Katie was the perfect teacher for John to learn how to handle anger directed at him, differently.

He saw it in their next heated conversation. He took a deep breath, reminded himself of our conversation. He asked questions, realized Katie was missing key information on an important topic, got her that information and tamed the beast. It felt like a miracle.

In our next conversation, Katie mentioned how different her interactions were with John. "He has gotten much better in his communication with me."

I just smiled.

STAY BIG. GET CURIOUS. BE PRESENT.

ATTITUDE ADJUSTMENT

Managing your boss is YOUR responsibility.
If you do it well, they appreciate it. You are not being a doormat for not fighting back all the time. This is about being smarter in a given situation with a given personality so that you can be more effective and happier.

"The person who stays grounded and centered has the power in any given situation."

~ **Mark J. Silverman**

My friend, Brett Culp, an inspiring international keynote speaker, was in an airport on the tall escalator when a big suitcase came bouncing down at him. He felt the fear in his body and realized he couldn't get out of the way. He was going to get knocked down the rest of the way.

Somehow, he got his foot on the suitcase and wedged it into the stair.

Disaster averted. Fear and anger were coursing through his veins when he saw a woman running towards him.

"I'm so sorry … that was all my fault, I'm glad you are okay."

Brett being the huge-hearted, aware guy that he is saw that the woman was more shaken than him (and he was pretty shaken). He did his inner work and turned his attention on her.

"Are YOU okay?"

"No, I'm having the worst day," she said, and burst into tears.

"Would you like a hug?"

She said yes and they both held each other and cried together. Yes, he's that guy.

Brett got out of himself and into the situation. He saw past the surface to what was really going on. He changed an almost disaster into a beautiful human connection.

If you can do that at work, or in a fight with your significant other … you change the game. So how does this work?

Just a note here. While I include understanding your job from your boss' point of view in this group of worksheets, that isn't part of this book.

MASTERING THE TRIGGER/RESPONSE

"I'm completely convinced, we are all operating out of our childhood selves. The people who are unconscious of it are the ones that are in the ditch all the time, because they keep falling prey to the same triggers.

Me, for example, despite the fact that I'm being told that I'm a worthless piece of you know what, from my father, I started meeting people, and just instinctively giving them what I didn't get. I wasn't really conscious of that in the beginning, but what I was conscious of was that I'm getting great results from people.

And it wasn't until I was in my 40s that somebody who worked for me for 20 years, pointed it out. She told me all the ways I was different from all the other managers, and how I treated people. I made what happened with my father a positive thing. It could have been a very negative thing, I could have been horrible to people, I could have passed on what I got, which is what most of us do. Somehow, I did the opposite."

Mark C. Crowley, author of *Lead From the Heart*
The Rising Leadership Podcast episode 22:
"Leading from the Heart"
https://bit.ly/3Rgl1ar

Let's take a moment and reflect on how your boss affects you.

What do you do, how do you act when your boss triggers you? Really take the time to notice what happens in your body, emotions, and thoughts.

Slow down the automatic cause and effect, change the game.

Athletes do drills so their muscle memory knows what to do when the time comes. Meditation is lifting weights for the mind and soul. Self-reflection is the same thing if you want to move from reaction to considered response.

Let's create a game plan BEFORE it happens.

Pause

If you can pause, you can uncover and respond to what is really happening rather react to what you "think" is happening.

Think of a time when you got triggered by your boss.
Take out a notebook for this one.
Try these sentence stems for your journaling:

What happened?
When my boss …
I felt …
I made it mean …
I acted in this way …
Now take a moment and consider if your initial perception
was accurate.

Reflect and Recover
Is what I made it mean true?
What could be truer?
If I didn't take it personally, how could I be different?
With your new perspective, and a moment to let the charge pass …

Respond
Take a breath. You are allowed to take a moment to recover
even in real time. You can now respond in a professional and
mature manner.

Kim Scott, author of *Radical Candor* puts it this way, "If you
are about to send an angry email and you are proud that it's a real
zinger, stop. If it feels too good, don't send it. Pause, reflect and
respond in a better way."

Homework

Think of three instances where your boss triggered you in
the past and work this self-inquiry on them. This practice
with the past will help you with the future. Do your reps.

Generally, if anyone gets angry (including you) more than a 4 or 5 (scale of 10) it isn't the situation. It's from the past. Don't take the bait. Don't take it personally.

> **THE PERSON WHO STAYS GROUNDED AND CENTERED HAS THE POWER IN ANY GIVEN SITUATION.**

Let's consider some more about leading up and how you can be more resilient, grounded and centered in every situation. We will revisit this in Leading You for a deeper dive.

For access to worksheets and other resources go to

https://bit.ly/46r8u8u

Chapter 2

SPEAKING YOUR MIND

"Those of us who study the fear of speaking in front of others believe it's innate to being human, we see it in every culture. We see it a rise mostly when kids enter into early teen years, and it stays with us. When you get up in front of others or put on the spot to speak, your heart races, your brow perspires, your mind gets a little jumbled. That's what we mean by fear of public speaking.

We believe this is part of our biology. As humans evolved, we would hang out in small groups, about 150 people. Your relative status in that group determined your access to food, shelter, and reproduction. Anything you do, that risks that status, like getting up in front of others and making a gaffe or saying the wrong thing in the wrong way, had pretty significant consequences. It's baked into who we are as humans. but that doesn't mean we can't learn to manage it.

What we know is that if people trust you and respect you, it helps. Listening is more important in persuading, then speaking. So trying to ask the right questions, showing that you're listening can be very, very important. When it comes to being influential, the most important thing you have to do is help people understand the relevance of what you're saying and appreciate the areas of resistance hesitation or concern that they might have that prevent them from acting.

Whenever you are trying to influence or persuade somebody, you have to think about two distinct approaches to take. One is to focus on all the reasons why they should do what you think they should do. We call those promoting messages. And then you also have to think about the restraining forces what prevents somebody from doing something. And sometimes the most effective, persuasive messages are the ones that remove restraining forces, rather than ones that just promote what you should do. I'll give you a quick example. When I went to grad school, I had a friend. We both graduated college same time, he went into the professional world right away, I went to grad school. Suffice it to say, he made a lot more money more quickly than me. I have not done as well.

When I was in grad school, he kept coming to me saying, "Hey, let's go let's go to Tahoe, let's go to Hawaii." I mean, he had this disposable income that I did not have. He would try to persuade me with all the great reasons for going to Hawaii, going to Tahoe. I understood all those reasons, the restraining force: I didn't have time, and I didn't have money. So, all of the promoting messages were just frustrating me, right? It's not that I didn't understand going to Hawaii is fun. I got that. It's ... I couldn't do it. So sometimes, the better persuasion is to actually target the things that prevent somebody from doing something and help equip them there. And that's what's going to get them to come to your side or be persuaded by what you're saying. So it all boils down to understanding your audience is listening, and then ultimately figuring out am I promoting or am I working on restraining forces?

I call it reconnaissance, reflection, and research ... you have to do all three of the three R's before you actually assert your point of view ... reconnaissance, reflection and research."

Matt Abrahams, author of *Think Faster Talk Smarter*
The Rising Leader Podcast episode 42:
"Mastering Spontaneous Public Speaking"
https://bit.ly/3RhK78X

We just spent an entire chapter focusing on how to get along with your boss, because we want you to be more effective. We want you to be trusted. We want you to be listened to when you have important input. Knowing your audience is the most powerful tool for influencing.

Building trust with your boss means you've earned the right to speak your mind when needed.

When you feel the need to speak up, keep in mind what my friend and mentor, life coach Diana Bonnici teaches:

Time. Place. Space.

Is it the right time to have this conversation?

Is it the right place to have this conversation?

Are all parties in the right (head) space to have this conversation?

Answering yes to all three will improve your chances of a positive impact. (Note: this goes for personal relationships as well)

If your goal is to become a trusted advisor, you are going to need to be trustworthy. Think about your own role and how every day is a gauntlet of business challenges, opportunities, and relationships to navigate. It seems everyone wants your attention, and everyone has an opinion. Multiply that by some number, and you get an idea of what your boss deals with.

Think about the people on your team who have earned your trust. They are probably good at what they do, handle problems on their own and only come to you when needed. And when they do, they come with the information you need and a solution or two.

There is another invaluable trait to YOUR trusted advisor. You KNOW they have your best interest in mind. They have your back. So, if they confront you, make a mistake, or disagree with you, you trust their "come from." You can deal with the issue directly because you don't have the baggage of "are they or aren't they on my side?"

It's more difficult to judge how we are showing up. We know our intention, but how is it landing? This is where the empathy map comes in handy. It humanizes your relationship. Slows it down. You can ask, and find out.

"Leadership is lonely."

~ **unknown**

You want to be that place where your boss feels they have an ally on a day when they feel like they are alone against the world.

Accomplishing this gives you the room to speak your mind, challenge, disagree etc.

I coach several people on a leadership team of a large company.

When speaking with the CEO of one of my client companies, they shared a very pointed and specific criticism of another executive client. He went on at length while I listened. Then he asked:

CEO: *"Do you get what I mean, Mark? (He was harshly criticizing his CFO, Emily.) I need you to coach her on this for me."*

Mark: *"I hear what you're saying, it's very clear. There is just one problem. I have interviewed Emily's peers and her team for her 360 review. They called out this specific weakness that you experience, as her zone of genius. They actually experience her differently."*

CEO: *"So, you're saying, it's me?"*

Mark: *"Yes ... and no. Yes, because she is actually great at this and no, because you and she are not connecting on this issue. That needs to happen. But I cannot teach it. It's your job to work with Emily to be more effective with you on this topic. Teach her how best to communicate with you."*

I can speak truth to the CEO. I am a trusted advisor for him. I am also not the CEO's coach. He has a damned good one. But he pays me a good chunk of change to coach his folks. It could cost me a lot if I got on his wrong side. And I have a few things going for me.

1. A commitment to speaking truth. It is a value of mine to be candid when needed and not worry about what it might cost me. It's served me well, (most of the time).

2. I am judicious in my "truth telling." When I speak, it's heard.

3. I have earned the CEO's trust over time. He knows I have his back. He knows if I am being confrontational, my "come from," has his, my client's, and his company's best interest.

This is what is available to you.

"I have some pet peeves. People who work with me and know me well know them well. For example, a long email. I hate long emails. I never send them and I hardly ever read them.

Somebody hits you with this email that's three pages long, am I going to block out the next 15 minutes of my day and reprioritize my schedule and revisit email, which I have to concentrate to really absorb at all, or am I going to just continue to do my job? There's a real art to saying less, and having it be memorable rather than just dumping the whole thing out there.

Another CEO I worked with, Frank Slootman would say, "I need clarity of thought." If people were running on too long, he would say, "Give me your main priorities netted out."

Kevin Haverty
The Rising Leader Podcast episode 13:
"Rising from Super Sales Rep to Effective Leader"
https://bit.ly/3MPXafp

Have you ever walked out of a leadership meeting shaking your head because no one spoke up about the bad idea the CEO just ran with? You would have spoken up, but everyone followed down the path with him/her, so you couldn't find the voice to disagree? I bet the answer is, "all too often."

It is easier (and safer) to be a "Yes-person" than an honest feedback person.

An insecure CEO shuts their team down. He turns them into an agreeable, frictionless group of order takers.

A confident CEO wants to hear a difference of opinion. She may not like it. She may not even take the guidance, but she wants thoughtful, honest feedback to make the best decision possible.

Mastery is being able to become the trusted advisor to a confident boss, or an insecure boss.

Let me give you two examples.

Sheryl is a driven, brilliant tech CEO. She built her company from nothing to 1.5 billion dollars in sales. Of course, she had a talented team of engineers building a killer product and a motivated sales team crushing their goals every quarter. But it was Sheryl who made sure the rocket ship over-achieved.

The executive team loved her and would follow her anywhere. If you go back to our boss types, Sheryl had her positives and she also had a temper. She leaned toward "rage-a-holic." She unwittingly shut down dissent on her team. Few disagreed with her in the leadership team meetings. The consequences of the lack of honest input were too easily overlooked by the success of the company. As long as the money was flowing, where was the problem?

Once in a while, Sheryl did make a decision, or pushed an initiative that had major negative impact. That is when everyone turned to Craig. Craig was the "Sheryl Tamer." He had her trust. He rarely disagreed but would step up when it was important.

He lived the Boss Empathy Map and knew how to communicate with her. He also only pushed back when it was necessary. If Craig needed to have a talk, Sheryl knew she should listen. Be like Craig.

If you can be that voice of reason when your boss is stressed, you've earned the title, Trusted Advisor.

How do you speak truth to power while supporting the CEO in their goals and vision?

You already started with the Boss Empathy Map, and your interview in the last chapter. You've created agreements and ground rules about disagreeing, giving feedback, and offering up possible pitfalls to a given initiative. You are creating trust. You have a good foundation.

As I mentioned above, most CEOs are Idea Machines. Their team are the Implementers. The CEO needs to be free to bring up initiatives, business opportunities, create new products and departments, weigh in on the progress of a project or one of your star people. Great visionaries are often unreasonable and audacious. They don't want to be bogged down in the "how" or "can't" until they need to be.

Your job is to be their eyes and ears — know the budgets, resources, people, market trends and any other factors that will affect their idea.

First, you need to decide what is important and what is not. You are going to need to trust yourself and your perspective.

Steve is the CFO and has been working with the CEO since they were a 4-person company. They are now 535 employees, and the company is still growing. In fact, the leadership team is now 12 people. Because they started the company together, Steve is very comfortable disagreeing with his boss, even in front of the entire leadership team. His personality type Enneagram 6, (which I'll discuss later) is one of seeing what will go wrong before anyone else. He is right much of the time. Steve forgets they are no longer an informal 4-person company. He forgets the CEO has a board to answer to, 535 people they feel responsible for, other people on the leadership team that must be considered and that while Steve is mostly HQ-based, the CEO spends 60% of their time in hotels and airports.

I was hired because Steve is a rock star, and Steve can be a pain in the ass with his constant warning of what can go wrong. His leadership skills, and his tact have not matured as fast as his responsibilities. It is awesome that he has no fear of speaking his mind, but it has turned into a negative at the new scale. Especially with the increased pressure on the CEO.

Steve had to learn to triage his relentless drive to bring everything to the CEO's attention. Not because it was bad but because the important got drowned out by the sheer volume from him and everyone else bringing problems that need solving. He was becoming noise instead of effective.

PICK A HILL TO DIE ON

"A way to get your point across and to say it very clearly is to use the three-question structure.

What? What is your point? It's your product, your service, idea, or belief.

Why? Why is it important to the people in the room or beyond?

What's next? Or now what? Set up another meeting? Take questions. Do research?

When I have to give an update or assert my point of view, I will say" here's my point of view, here's why it's important, and here's what I think we should do about it."

Matt Abrahams, author of *Think Faster Talk Smarter*
The Rising Leader Podcast episode 42:
"Mastering Spontaneous Public Speaking"
https://bit.ly/3RhK78X

We all have only so much political capital in any group of people. Being on a leadership team is a prime example. Your effectiveness depends on the good will deposits you make with the team and how well you can read the room. It is even more precious when dealing with your boss.

- Loyalty/trust
- Performance/results
- Insight

- Problem-solving
- Cheerleading

Contribute to your status as trusted advisor.

- Breaking trust
- Missing goals/breaking agreements
- Complaining
- Negativity

Destroy your standing.

But you know this. The blind spot or trap many high achievers fall into is thinking they are being helpful by bringing up everything that is "wrong." You feel "on top of it," and that you are being helpful by not letting things fall through the cracks.

By taking this shotgun approach, you unknowingly become a person to avoid. Your good intention starts to feel negative *even though it is not.* Steve, who I mentioned above, was falling into that trap.

Your job as trusted advisor is to do triage on all that is happening in the organization, that you feel compelled to address, and move from shotgun to rifle. Narrow down your focus, everyone's attention, and resources to those things that need to get addressed first.

STEVE'S COACHING

"You gotta pick a hill to die on. You can't take every hill."

"But these things are important, Mark, and people are dropping the ball."

"Maybe so, but if everything is important, nothing is important. Better said, the entire team, including the CEO are tuning you out. You are overloading them and becoming noise."

"But…"

"Do you want to be right, or do you want to be effective, because you have complained that people are not listening to you."

After a much longer conversation (several, actually) he saw it. He also saw how he was driving himself crazy, building resentments, losing sleep, and working himself to exhaustion because of his hyper vigilance.

Side Note: The CEO has the same personality type as Steve, fear-based and looks for what can go wrong. With Steve pointing out every rock in the harbor, the CEO was having meltdowns, sure of a shipwreck, in response to Steve's good intention.

Let's pick on Steve a little more.

We did a 360-degree feedback session on Steve and one topic that came up is that he is called "Dr. No" by the others on the team. A hard pill to swallow.

To be fair, Steve's job as CFO was to be conservative and guard the company's financial and legal interests.

If your job is CFO or Legal Counsel, you may find yourself saying "No," a lot. Even if your job is literally to be a speed bump, you will be more effective if you up-level your communication. When giving feedback like this it is important to be honest and direct, resistance is natural, but if the recipient shuts down you have a ton of work to do to gain trust and get moving again.

You are good at your job because you are good at keeping order, setting up guard rails, and fighting for what you think is right. The problem is that the CEO and the rest of the team are running a business.

YOUR 'COME FROM' IS "BE SAFE."
THEIR 'COME FROM' IS "WHAT'S POSSIBLE?"

The first helpful shift is to look at things from their perspective. The best way to learn is though conversation.

The second is the language you use. Instead of "no," try "we could do this but it will conflict with this SEC statute. I looked and cannot find a way around it."

Or, "There are legal issues with the way you want to do this, but if you can modify in this way, we can make it work."

That way, you build a reputation for being "on the team." When you do need to bring a hard "no," it will carry more weight.

Let's get back to Steve.

We did a verbal Empathy Map so Steve could understand the CEOs new world. The one he had never considered as the company (and the leadership team) grew.

They are tired from all the travel.

The CEO is still the best closer in the company.

They have 10 "Leaders" with ideas, complaints, needs, and personalities.

They now have a board and investors with cell phones and opinions.

They are constantly in front of cameras evangelizing.

Trade magazines evaluate the company's progress, employee satisfaction, diversity and inclusion practices.

Message boards posts by disgruntled (right or wrong) employees.

It sunk in. The feedback, the conversations, the empathy, and the newly-acquired skills helped Steve become more effective ... and he enjoyed his day a lot more.

You may not be Dr. No but you may have your rough edges.

Are you the "everything is important, everything needs to be done right or not done at all" type?

Are you really attached to your version of right?

Are you quieter and self-conscious, and the CEO has to pull opinions out of you?

We all can be a pain in the ass … figure out your flavor and make sure you haven't turned your gift into a negative.

HOW TO DECIDE WHICH HILL TO TAKE

Use this exercise to determine what is actually worth your time, energy, resources, and political capital.

If you are like Steve and firehose your opinions, let's focus your impact.

If you are quieter, let's decide where you need to push yourself to speak up.

DEFINE THE IMPACT

My Important Thing	Impact On Me, The Organization, Resources Needed?
My Important Thing	Impact On Me, The Organization, Resources Needed?
My Important Thing	Impact On Me, The Organization, Resources Needed?

1. Write down all the things that need to be changed, improved, or fixed in your organization.

2. Which ones impact you, your goals or responsibilities?

3. Which ones impact the organization in a significant way?

4. If you could only make ONE change at this time, which would it be?

    Got it?

5. Assuming that ONE thing is handled ... what would your next ONE thing be?

   Got it?

6. Assuming that NEXT ONE thing is handled ... what would your next ONE thing be?

   Got it?

7. Rewrite your list of three things and leave room for notes.

   Discover the impact:

8. Next to each ONE thing answer the following questions:

   » Is it my responsibility or someone else's?

   » If someone else's (need to revisit) ...

   » What is the impact on me or my team (of addressing or not addressing)?

   » What is the impact on the organization (of addressing or not addressing)?

   » What resources will be needed to address this item?

   » Worth it (in the context of everything else)?

Choosing can be hard, when you choose something to work on, you are choosing not to work on something else. Again, when we get to personality types and motivations you will learn that choosing is difficult for different reasons for everyone. Knowing the underlying stressor of your particular personality trait helps in the decision making.

Now that you have your three hills, we can get laser-focused on getting something accomplished.

Go ahead and list out your three things. You now know where to focus. But first, we have to do a little more work.

"I am not right; I have a perspective." This will be your humility mantra. This has you go into a meeting with an open mind.

Do you know how this impacts other team members? Have you spoken to them?

What is the impact on the CEO, your Team, other Team Leads?

When you have an understanding of the playing field, you will understand better how it may be received in the communication, and how to adjust your communication.

Your job is to influence. Hone your "Enrollment Skills."

Once you are clear, your priority list can be a topic of conversation in your regular meetings with your boss, peers, and team.

"This is what I am focused on this week."

STACKING THE DECK – THE MEETING BEFORE THE MEETINGS

"Most discussions should happen before you go into the boardroom. Before you walk in, you should meet with the stake holders one by one. You should always know where they are coming from and how your idea impacts them. There should be no surprises."

Tom Mendoza
The Rising Leader Podcast episode 30:
"People-Centered Leadership"
https://bit.ly/3GBX3Rb

I call this "Stacking the Deck." It is the meeting before the meeting when you have something important you want to present, an idea you want implemented or support you (or your division) need, and you bring it to the leadership team meeting. The benefits or stacking the deck are that:

- Nobody likes to be surprised

- Stakeholders need time to consider anything that affects them or their team

- Objection handling ahead of time

- Know the playing field before you present

In an article on podcast interviewing skills, the author mentioned an interview I conducted on *The Rising Leader Podcast*. He made this observation: "Notice when Mark asked this question. It was clear he had done his research and already knew the answer. Knowing how the guest would answer helped Mark expertly steer the conversation exactly where he wanted it to go."

My sales training never leaves me.

Do your homework. The investment will pay dividends.

FOUNDATION FOR SPEAKING UP

Speaking up is risky. In order to do so, you need to have a strong foundation that gives you the confidence to take on that risk.

First, let's check on your reputation.

⇨ Are you known as a team player?

⇨ Do you consistently create results?

⇨ Supportive of others?

Second ... have you ever noticed politicians who are desperate to stay in office will do and say anything to keep their job?

Never allow yourself to be in survival mode.

"In some cases, it works. And in some cases, it doesn't. I can recall an instance where I was the Chief Operating Officer of a multi-$100 million plus organization where the CEO and I did not see eye to eye. This was during the early 2000s, around the .com bust. Myself and another gentleman had pitched a business idea to our parent company on building this consultancy organization. We built the organization from 75 to over

1500 people in a span of six months. The bubble burst, just after that, and we had to downsize the company more than half. We did an in-person all hands meeting, (there were no virtual meetings then.) I got up in front of the team and explained to them that, although it was difficult, and a lot of our friends were no longer in the organization that we had cut to the bone. We had to right size to move forward and grow the business.

A week later, the CEO called me, "Michael, I think we need to cut more." To be fair, his orientation was manufacturing and mine was services. I believed people were an asset.

I said, "We can't cut deeper, and if you do, you're going to disrupt the business. But if that's the decision you've made, then you need to put my name on the top of that list of the people that you're going to let go." I felt my personal integrity with the team was at stake.

He gladly accepted my resignation. After that, they had a mass exodus. But I'm happy to say today that was the origins of what is Hitachi consulting. I'm proud I had a had a hand in creating that business that is a billion dollar plus today.

You have to be authentic, and you have to be true to your convictions. Sometimes those convictions can be career limiting. But I'm a firm believer that, you know, we have a bigger calling in life than just profitability of an organization.

Mark: "How has it served you since that experience?"

That experience gave me the confidence that I could be a courageous leader. There are people today that were in that environment and still believed that was the right thing to do. I also received the benefit of their trust, loyalty and commitment. I've actually hired some of those people in other organizations along the way. That is important to me.

As a leader, you have to have the confidence in your ability to be successful, regardless of where you are or the situation. I think it would have been more detrimental for me to step away from my core values than it was to make that hard decision to say, "you need to put me on that list."

People who work for me say, "Michael, we always know where you stand. You always are an advocate for your team, for your customers, and for doing what's right for the business."

Michael D. Robinson, Vice President Healthcare VMware
The Rising Leader Podcast episode 23:
"Leadership, Authenticity, Accountability and Values"
https://bit.ly/3SUIe3p

OUR SENSE OF WELL-BEING IS IN DIRECT PROPORTION TO THE NUMBER OF OPTIONS WE FEEL WE HAVE.

If we are in survival for our job, we won't speak up.

Speaking up takes courage. Every difficult conversation we talk about in this book comes with risk.

Have you ever watched *Office Space?* In the movie the main character, Peter Gibbons, hates his job and is actively looking to get fired.

He is regularly brought in to meet with company representatives (both named Bob) and gets grilled for his "opinion." Because he doesn't care, he tells it like it is. And gets promoted. The more he criticizes the company the more "The Bobs" like him and he gets promoted again.

It's a classic, I recommend it for your next movie night.

I had my own relationship with "The Bobs" when I was a start-up guy in the tech world. It is regular occurrence in that world for larger companies to purchase smaller ones. One large company, we dubbed, The Evil Machine Company (true story) purchased three separate start-ups I worked at. By the third time, the running joke was, "Silverman, where are you going next so we know which company to buy next?" When it was announced, I immediately stated that I would leave at the end of the fiscal year. Even though I hated the Evil Machine Company, I wanted to be loyal to my current manager, who I liked and respected and didn't want to leave him in a lurch. I was way too honest, though, "I'm gone as soon as I get that last commission check."

"What can we do to make you stay?" VPs would ask my opinion on all sorts of topics. I had never been treated so well. I had the power.

In hindsight, I probably should have stayed because my next move was not so prescient. In fact, it sucked. It took two more leaps to hit it right again. Every action involves a risk. I am grateful that I always made sure I had the support to live my values.

If you have that courage, great. If not, I have some questions for you.

- How's your resume?
- LinkedIn Profile?
- Is your network robust and tended to?
- When was the last time you went on a job interview?
- How are your savings?

Even if you love your job, feel secure, and have no reason to be looking over your shoulder, you need to know your worth. You need to understand the market and your place in it. Make sure you are having a beverage of your choice with someone on the regular. Stay connected.

This helps in speaking your mind and while asking for a raise, benefits, or setting a boundary. It's time to take stock.

ENROLLMENT SKILLS

Everything is sales. Everything. If you want to go on a date, have your idea followed, or get your two-year-old to eat her peas … you must learn to influence.

I get a lot of push back on this.

"I hate playing politics."

"They don't listen to me; they listen to so and so who is a brown noser."

"Why do I have to fight for resources, it's their company?"

When I was in corporate my whine was, "Why do I have to sell to my boss, my company, our partners AND my customers all the time?"

The answer is ... "because you do." The world is noisy and needy, and you need to take responsibility for being heard.

"I would form coalitions when I needed to get something done. It's easier to get concepts passed when you have your peers singing on the same sheet of music. You just don't go in with an idea fresh out of the gate, you really have to do a lot of building.

The job is more about influence than anything else. Everything is a negotiation.

Everybody's coming in with their own agenda and fears. You have to address their desires and fears.

Once you build credibility, it's easier to convince people because success breeds success. But that first big initiative you undertake is usually the hardest, because you have to build that trust.

It's okay to lose, everything's a learning experience. It could have been the timing or it wasn't presented it right. There may be other things that are going on in the organization that you don't know about. Don't lose hope. You will have an opportunity to bring it up again.

You have to change your language as you move up. You are talking to people that have business problems vs technical. I talk technology, their eyes would glaze over and I wouldn't get anywhere. I needed to talk in language that they understood.

What were the business impacts of what I was doing? What did it what did it mean to them? How did it impact them. Your language has to change every level you go up.

The interesting thing is, you still need to speak in your old language to your team, create a new language for your peers and your superiors. That's the hardest thing to do.

You have to assimilate and translate the information.

I've failed too, I've tried to get approval for things that people looked at me like, Are you crazy, you're not talking my language. I'd have to take a second pass and maybe even a third pass to get it done properly. You keep going back better and with more clarity."

Beth Perlman, Managing Director, Chief Information Officer Advisor, Think Consulting
The Rising Leader Podcast episode 20:
"Being Influential as a Leader"
https://bit.ly/3uFaU69

ATTITUDE ADJUSTMENT

Know and accept that it is your job to
"sell the ecosystem on your ideas and solutions."

If you want your ideas to have impact, you have to navigate

- Multiple personalities
- Multiple agendas
- Multiple responsibilities
- Multiple fears
- Limited resources

This book's primary goal is to up-level your influence through skills and relationships. One of the best tools at your disposal is to let go of your ego. Try your best to separate YOU from your ideas. Let go of the way things *should* be, take 100% responsibility if things don't go your way.

We spend so much energy on the injustice of it all that we aren't at full capacity to address the reality of it all.

A general rule response:

- If your boss says no—is it a hill worth dying on? If not, they're the boss. Let it go.
- If the team says no—do they know something you don't know? Did you do your prework? If it's worth fighting for, it's worth building a better case.
- You feel ignored—how are you showing up? Do you greet every person in the meeting before it starts? Deep breath, respectfully take your space.
- Speak up: "Excuse me just a moment, I have something to add on that last point."

They say, "Dumb baseball players are the best players, because they let go of the last at bat and focus on the current one."

Let go of losses, don't hold grudges, face forward.

GIVING YOUR BOSS FEEDBACK

"First, build trust. Second, be honest, in your feedback. If it's if it's negative feedback, I find that that's always delivered best in private, you don't want to drop a bomb on your boss's desk in a meeting and suck all the oxygen out of the room. There are times when it's appropriate for the whole team to be involved in the problem solving. But if there's something going on, that needs correction or needs addressing, nine times out of 10, that should be a private conversation. By the way, that's how trust is built."

Kevin Haverty
The Rising Leader Podcast 13:
"Rising from Super Sales Rep to Effective Leader"
https://bit.ly/3MPXafp

When I asked Kim Scott about giving feedback on *The Rising Leader Podcast* she said: "Before you can dish it out, make sure you can take it. Ask for feedback, listen, and demonstrate a willingness to act on that feedback if it is useful. Then your feedback will be more easily heard. You will create a culture of candid feedback." You can hear more of this discussion "The Art of Radical Candor" episode https://bit.ly/3RgOO2T.

Your boss needs an honest sounding board and a catcher for blind spots. You can only be that person if you have created trust in all the ways we have discussed.

They need feedback on:

○ Their impact

○ Their ideas

○ The health of the organization (ear to the ground)

Pick your hills wisely. Check that you have your boss' and the company's best interests at heart. Remember, your boss is also human.

Also remember your "Know Your Boss" clarity. Have you had the feedback/disagreement conversation?

"I want to be a valued voice for you. I'm curious, if I disagree with you, what is the best way for me to share that? If I want to give you feedback, what is the best way you can hear that?"

REMEMBER:
TIME, PLACE, SPACE.

Be clear and concise:

- What is the factual/observable thing that happened?
- The impact was …
- Pause for response or question.
- Offer to offer a perspective or solution.

Keep notes.

Keep on track.

Keep brief.

Pro tip – It is more than okay to speak from notes when having a difficult conversation. You can even say, "I want to be precise, so I made some notes

SITUATIONAL SPEAKING UP

When Matt Abrahams was on *The Rising Leader Podcast*, I asked him to play "rapid fire situational communication" with me. Here is a sampling of what we learned.

"I don't think we ever truly can overcome our anxiety. I think there is always a situation that can make us nervous when it comes to speaking. In fact, having a little anxiety is a good thing. It gives you energy, helps you focus, and tells you what you're doing is important.

When it comes to managing anxiety, you have to take a two-pronged approach, you have to manage symptoms, and sources. So, what you just shared is, is it's hard to breathe, your heart rate starts beating really fast, some of us sweat and blush, that's what happens to me, others shake. And there's some things we can do to manage those symptoms. But they're also sources, things that initiate and exacerbate our anxiety. So happy to talk about those more. But the reality is, we can do something to feel better about our anxiety around speaking.

There is this mindset of perception deficit, I call it the field real divide. What you feel is not always what people see. That's the first mindset. The second mindset is that it's not about you. Many of us get very self-absorbed when we speak. We're worried about us. Psychologists have identified it as the spotlight effect, where we feel the spotlights on us and everybody's focusing on us. The reality is everybody is walking around this planet with spotlights on themselves. They're more focused internally than externally. Remember, it's not about you, it's about your audience. If you can have this mindset shift of, "I'm going to appear more confident than I feel", and "I have value to bring to my audience," rather than all the things that you focus on yourself you will be in a better place to speak. When you find yourself worried about what you need to say, the most important question you should ask is, what does the audience need to hear?

For symptomatic relief, deep belly breaths are incredibly important. What's interesting about deep belly breaths, like if you're doing yoga, or tai chi, is it's the exhale that's most important. If you take a three count in, take a six count out, so if you double your exhale, to your inhale, it will help. You only have to do it two or three times. We also need to remember to practice."

ON SPONTANEOUS SPEAKING

"In reality, a lot of what we do in our day-to-day life is spontaneous. Somebody asks a question, somebody asked for feedback, you make a mistake, you have to fix it in the moment.

In that moment, a couple things can help. One, remind yourself that this isn't a threat, it is an opportunity. This is an opportunity to explore, to collaborate, it could be a gateway to amazing things for you. But if you go and say, it's wrong, it should be this way, it's unprofessional, you get defensive, not only in your physical posture, but your tone is curt, your answers are short.

If instead, you go in and say, "Hey, all right, here I am. I have an opportunity, it's an adventure, let's see what happens. That open mindset can help."

ON BEING PUT ON THE SPOT

"I have a colleague at the business school, Collins Dobbs, he's a great guy. He has this notion that he uses when you're having high impact, high intensity conversations. He calls it pace, space, grace. I've adapted his approach to listening. Part of pace is you have to slow things down. Space, you have got to give yourself a little distance to really think through what you're thinking. Then you have to give yourself a little grace.

There are three ways one can create space. You can pause. Many of us feel very uncomfortable pausing, but it is normal and natural. Second, you can ask clarifying questions. If you are asked, "why did this failure happen? And what's going on?" You could ask, "are you talking about this last month or the course of the year?" Not only does that help me better understand what you need, again, we want to be in service of our audience, but it also gives me time to think. A third way is to be paraphrase what you've heard. Again, it shows you are listening and gives you time.

Many of us feel compelled ... we have to respond immediately. And you can take a little beat. I'm not taking saying take 10 minutes, I'm saying take a couple seconds, collect your thoughts."

ON IF YOU DON'T KNOW

"Of course, you may not know the answer. Say, "I do not know." But immediately follow it up with what you'll do to find out and tell them the timeframe you'll get back. If you have a hunch or an inkling let them know. "What you're really asking about is the core issue that brought around about this potential failure? I don't know the exact answer. I'm going to get back with my team. By end of day tomorrow, I'll have an answer. My hunch is it has to do with the system protocols that we just implemented. I'll confirm."

ON IF YOU DRAW A BLANK WHILE SPEAKING

"If you can't remember what to say, and you want to say something, a couple things you can do. One, go back to go forward. If you lose your keys, how do you find them? You retrace your steps. If I'm in the midst of speaking and I blank out, just repeat what you just said. Most of us can remember what we just said it gets us back on track.

The other thing you can do is ask a question to buy yourself time. If somebody asked me a question, I don't know how to answer, I ask a question that distracts them effectively, so I can get back on track. I do this all the time, when I teach. Sometimes I can't remember if I said that in this class or was at the other class. In those moments, when I need just to think a little bit more, I'll just stop and say, "I'd like to pause, I'd love for you to think about how what we've just discussed can be applied in your life." My students aren't thinking, *Oh, Matt forgot,* my students were thinking, *wow, how do I apply this in my life.* You can do this to remind yourself if you blank out."

ON WEDGING YOURSELF INTO A CONVERSATION

"If there's a lot of conversation going on, and you want to wedge your voice into that conversation, three things you can do.

Paraphrasing is key. If I want to wedge my voice in, I can simply paraphrase something you said, "Mark you are saying..." and I just summarize your point. That gives me a wedge or an entry point. I can ask a question. I can also lead with emotion, "I'm excited about that because..." It gives you permission to put your voice into the conversation."

Matt Abrahams
The Rising Leader Podcast episode 42:
"Mastering Spontaneous Public Speaking"
https://bit.ly/3RhK78X

For access to worksheets and other resources go to
https://bit.ly/46r8u8u

Chapter 3

DOING YOUR JOB

"Once in a while, you need to step back and give some thought on how you're spending your time because when you get in a bigger job, you could work 24 hours a day and not get everything done. It's not a matter of working harder. You really can't work harder. It's a matter of choosing what I am going to work on and how many hours I will work on it. You do need to shut it down, you do need to get your rest, you do need to get your exercise, you need to take care of yourself. Because if you just jumped on everything all the time you'd burn out.

I think the important thing on triaging is, be thoughtful. I'll give you an example. A few years ago, ServiceNow came up with the top 10 priorities for the corporation, and then they built committees for each. I got put on all 10 committees. I said, "Timeout, do you want me to run sales or do you want me to be a professional committee person, because if I'm on these 10 committees, I don't have much time for anything else. So pick two.

They had good intentions for wanting me on those committees but I wasn't having it. They came back with four, and I came back and said, "Pick two." You need to think about what are the things that are important to you and your job.

There's also a little bit of, what do I like to do? When you get to a certain level, you can pick and choose, and you're not going to pick things that are gonna make you miserable all the time.

Then there's also, where can I add value? Where can my skills benefit the company? If I'm spending time on something where it's just taking up my time, and I'm not really contributing, I'm wasting my own time, and I'm not really helping the company.

That helps you look at your schedule and decide, can I make an impact here? Is this something I like to do? And, you know, is this something that benefits of company?

If not, learn how to say no, in a constructive way. "I can't do that. Why don't you talk with so and so who works for me, they could probably represent my voice there." As you get better at that, I think that's when you really get better at being a productive leader."

Kevin Haverty
The Rising Leader Podcast episode 13:
"Rising from Super Sales Rep to Effective Leader"
https://bit.ly/3MPXafp

GETTING CLARITY

CLARITY = EFFECTIVENESS

To be an effective trusted advisor and to stay out of overwhelm, you need to get clarity on your official and unofficial roles and responsibilities. It's time to understand your job from your boss' point of view.

Your boss' job is to be clear with you. Few are good at it. That means your job is to get the clarity for yourself.

My guess is you could not work any harder than you are now. Like most of my clients, you are hyper-responsible, willing to help at a moment's notice, and have the missed family time to show for it.

If you are going to work this hard, shouldn't you make sure you are working on the right things?

- Get clear on what you are officially and unofficially measured on so that you know where you need to focus your time and energy in order to get the results you are responsible for.

- Identify where your time goes and how long you actually spend on Internal and External Distractions, and how long you spend on tasks that matter.

- Manage and minimize your Internal and External Distractions by becoming more aware and setting clear boundaries around your time and energy with your peers and team.

- Take ownership: learn how to focus your "visionary" boss with Agreements Conversations.

Get Out Your Calendar

If you cannot recall how you spend your days in detail you will need to keep a log of how you spend your time for one to three days. Think of yourself keeping track of "billable" hours. Understand and categorize how you spend your time.

Okay, get out your calendar or your log, it's time to take stock.

In an earlier chapter I suggested you interview your boss to find out what they think you should focus on. You know all too well that their perspective may be different from your job description. In many ways you will be evaluated, judged, and seen through this lens.

Unfortunately, your boss may not even know, on a day-to-day level, what you do for the organization.

"There is visible work and invisible work.
You get judged by the visible work."

~Helen Appleby, author of
The Unwritten Rules of Women's Leadership

As we see in the chart above, there are three lenses you need to be conscious of. The best way to do this is to get them on paper (or pixels).

Take the info you gathered over the past few days in your worksheet, and marry that to the chart below.

The Job You Were Hired to Do	The Job You Actually Do	The Job Your Boss Wants You to Do (Remember, You Asked)
- What is your actual job description?	- How would you describe your job?	- What does your boss need you to do?
- What Are You Measured On?	- What do you actually do every day (track list)?	- What do THEY think your job description is?

Take careful notice of how you are measured in your reviews and on what basis you get paid. If what you do with your time is a distraction from the objectives that will count, you have a problem. If your boss has you focused on some of these "distractions," it is time for a conversation.

This exercise should clear up any confusion you are feeling. Getting conscious of the forces that pull you in seemingly different directions at once is your first step to taking control of your destiny, your calendar and focus. It will also help you move from resentment and overwhelm to action.

From this place of clarity, you can have conversations and shift responsibilities, get resources, and become more effective in actual and perceived impact.

How much time are you spending working behind the scenes on things that do not further your cause? When you look at what you really do and what your boss wants you to do, it may be different from what you are paid and measured on.

Let's go back to your clarity conversation from earlier in the book. Where are the discrepancies from what you learned there and what you actually do?

Let's say you are the Chief Revenue Officer and have the below official job description.

Example: Chief Revenue Officer (CRO)
Description: Focus on strategic planning, marketing, branding, partnerships to generate increasing revenue streams.
Partner with senior leadership to execute the company's revenue generating plan.
Manage global sales team to drive business growth.

As CRO you will be measured on increasing revenue streams.

If the numbers aren't there, you do not have a job.

What is the job you find yourself doing day-to-day? You may have a list of responsibilities you should be doing, but my guess, is there are things you do every day that are outside that list.

Back to you as CRO. Let's say you must partner with a weak CMO (Marketing). You are not getting the effective campaigns needed to drive revenue. You may need to sit in on meetings to help focus a team that does not belong to you. Maybe the CMO isn't a effective leader and needs mentoring. There are any number of things you must do outside your job that supports her objective and you just have to do it or it won't get done.

I'm sure you can relate. What do you do on the regular that is unseen, but necessary. Maybe you are the Chief Psychologist that keeps the team from falling apart. Maybe you spearhead the annual philanthropic direction. Document it.

Then there is what your boss needs you to do. The list is endless here, especially if you are a trusted member of the inner circle.

- Sounding board for ideas and grievances
- Fix-it person for weak team members
- Float trial balloons for decisions
- Unofficial communications director

Consider if this is the third company where you have worked with the CEO.

You understand him, aren't afraid of him and can talk him off the ledge when needed. You, as CRO, have a mountain of responsibilities, but one of the most important is unofficial. You are trusted and can speak truth to power. This makes you invaluable.

WHAT ARE YOU UNOFFICIALLY MEASURED ON?

This varies from organization to organization. Values, culture and often, the CEO's preferences determine how your success is viewed. I've seen all kinds of things show up as plusses and minuses in a 360-feedback answer. Some healthy, some not so much.

- All hands-on deck (company over personal time)
- First to answer a text or email
- Braggers get valued (style over substance)
- Loyalty
- Amicability
- Act first (company or customer's interest) ask questions later
- Yes Man/Woman/Person
- Social Status
- Performance trumps bad behavior

You know your company's unofficial measuring tape. The art is to be aware of it, but not trapped by it. Remember what your boss values, and gear communication in that direction. It's not politics, it's being smart.

Now you are clear on what you should be doing to get your official job done, you know how you are measured and how you get paid. You know what you need to do unofficially to be in good standing with the tribe and the chief. Let's work on that balancing act.

CREATING BALANCE, FOCUS, AND EFFECTIVENESS

Your job is to create balance. If fixing someone else's work (even if the CEO is asking) is affecting your work, your family, or your mental health, it's time to speak up. Your ego may be a problem here. It can be a dopamine rush to be the person who always turns things around. Be careful of that.

Your boss may even balk at your negotiations and boundary setting. You have to keep moving the needle toward a sane workload where you are most effective where needed.

DISTRACTIONS:

Internal Distractions: The stuff in your head that keeps you from focusing on your job.

External Distractions: Everything in your world that keeps you from focusing on your job.

Internal Distractions:

- Playing the hero – looking good
- Dopamine hits – fun, visible, unimportant
- People pleasing – inability to say no
- Wanting to be liked – all the above

Look at the list of Internal Distractions above. Take some time to consider why you do those things. In Leading You, we will explore more how you can break your patterns of doing too much to quiet the voices in your head.

External Distractions: (often driven by internal distractions)

- Your boss is an idea machine – and you catch every one without discernment.
- You are the go-to person for your peers and team – you may love being the hero or afraid to say no.
- Doing your team's job – doing not leading.

You may be on to me by now. It's all "inner distractions." In *Only 10s*, I write, "If you are overwhelmed, you are doing someone else's job."

This means you are falling prey to habits and conditioning that keep you from doing effective triage, setting boundaries, creating workable agreements, and having difficult conversations.

HOW TO FOCUS UNDER FIRE

The chaotic needs of the organization, the constant fires, the "Hey, you got a minute?" interruptions, will have you lose sight of your actual job. You can never work hard enough to satisfy this bottomless pit of need.

You must put that white horse back in the stable until you know when and where you choose to be the hero. This is boundary setting 101. To set boundaries (like speaking up) you need to find your self-worth.

Are you willing to accept:

- That you cannot be ALL things to ALL people?
- That you cannot be the go-to person for EVERYTHING and EVERYONE?

Let's take a deep breath and reflect a moment.

Do you currently get your self-worth from being indispensable? Do you want a life, health, and balance or do you want burnout?

Are you currently knocking it out of the park on your actual job? Your family? Your well-being?

One of the most profound conversations I have had about burnout, particularly for woman was with Dr. Mandy Lehto. As a success-oriented overachiever, Mandy was all things to all people, and she did it all well. Until she couldn't.

Mark to Mandy: "So what was the turning point?"

Mandy: "There were several. But I think sometimes really smart people are extraordinarily stupid. The first was when my son was born. And I had to go back to work when he was 16 weeks old. And it tore my heart out because I wanted to spend more time with him.

The second one was when my marriage fell apart because I was never around. And there was a lot of tension. And that should have been a wake-up call too but I thought, no, no, I'm not there yet. I still need to keep pursuing this. And the story I told myself was that my then-husband just couldn't handle my success.

And the third thing that finally ended up pulling the rug out from under me was my body gave up. And this I think, had been going on for some time, but I didn't want to listen to it. So I was getting increasingly tired. But I mean, that kind of lifestyle where you're constantly reacting, meeting to meeting phone call to phone call, long hours, never really being able to switch off. I just thought that was normal because everybody that I surrounded myself with felt like that, too.

And little by little this exhaustion started to become more crippling. There were days where I just couldn't get out of bed. I was literally Velcroed to the bed. I thought, how can I face another day?

The doctor and they said, "There's nothing wrong with you."

[I said] there's nothing wrong with me. I just need more coffee. I need more coffee, I need more carbs. And I need more cardio, three theories that had kept me going for such a long time. So I hired a personal trainer and we doubled down.

Let's do some high-intensity cardio. He said, "Let's do something called high-intensity interval training." And the thing that actually broke the camel's back was boxing, because I said [to the trainer], is there anything there that has a bit more juice than this?

So we did boxing. Then all of a sudden, after about four minutes into one session, he said "let's do the left side now." I just dropped like a shot bird. And I was hunched over. I was foaming at the mouth. I was embarrassed. You know, my first thought was I was embarrassed for the trainer to see me like this because he wouldn't think I was strong. And that's one thing I had never been – weak.

I'm in this place of my body is in revolt. And my head is like what there's nothing wrong with me what is going on? The only thing that made me listen was I broke out in this hideous, oozing cracking rash that basically made it look like I had a goatee made of cornflakes."

Dr. Mandy Lehto, executive coach and host, *Enough the Podcast*
Mastering Midlife Podcast episode 3:
"Sustainable Success for the Achieving Woman"
https://bit.ly/3SPxmU6

Can you let go of getting your self-worth from driving yourself into the ground?

It took me years, but I did it. You can too. It starts with a decision. It is lived one conversation at a time.

"Self-esteem allows you to walk into a room, command a crowd, speak confidently. Self-value is the private decisions you make for yourself, how you treat yourself. Being raised as a child with self-confidence I never really addressed the self-value piece."

Valari Jackson, Keynote Speaker
Mastering Overwhelm Podcast episode 3:
"Self-Esteem vs Self-Worth"
https://bit.ly/3SXscpi

SETTING BOUNDARIES – CREATING NEW AGREEMENTS

I am going to ask you to look at what you can do to change the circumstances. You do not have to take action on any of these things. Just get them on paper so you can choose a hill to take.

Let's try one test case before you commit to the path of setting yourself free.

1 – Where do you need to set boundaries with your peers? Be specific on what you need to have change, what workable looks like, and who you need do speak with? List everyone out so you can see how much is on your plate ... that shouldn't be.

Some things will not be able to change ... done right, a good portion will shift.

Over time you can address the rest.

2 – Where do you need to set boundaries, build accountability and new agreements, with your team? Who do you need to step up? List them out so you can see where lack of leadership and accountability is costing you.

NOT MY CIRCUS, NOT MY MONKEYS

You can't fix everything. Nor should you try to.

Byron Katie, who I quote often, separates the world into three spheres of influence.

She says, "There is my stuff, your stuff, and G-d's stuff. I can only take care of my stuff."

We are going to change this up a bit for our purposes.

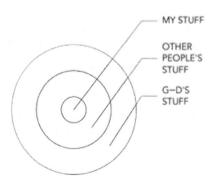

MY STUFF

OTHER PEOPLE'S STUFF

G–D'S STUFF

Imagine another diagram your stuff, your peers' stuff, and your organization's stuff. The organization's stuff belongs to the CEO and all the other people working there. They need jobs too.

Remember the hills you chose to take from the last section?

Marry that with the monkeys in this section. If you're focused on something that needs attention and resources, make sure it doesn't belong to someone else. If it does, your mantra is: "Not my circus, not my monkeys."

Focus on to your monkeys.

Note: Almost everyone I coach at your level is what I call hyper-responsible. You care, that's why you are a fast-rising, high achiever. You probably care too much. So much so, that it keeps you up at night and has you sacrificing for the good of your career. When I ask you to care less, I'm assuming this is true about you. I am trying to shock you into right sizing your effort so you can focus and be more effective.

Only committed high achievers get to use this mantra. You are one… so, "not my circus, not my monkeys."

You will always jump in when you need to jump in.

And I know all this is easier said than done. Make the effort.

Taming the human mind is like trying to
calm a drunk monkey stung by a scorpion.

~Chinese proverb

Let's explore the drunk monkeys creating a circus of their own in our head (internal distractions) that is keeping you off of your game.

Reflect

- When are you worried just to be worried (by habit)? (Hello, Enneagram 6 – Loyal Sceptic)

- When are you confusing passion for impact? Just because you care, doesn't mean you should.

- Where is the ideal slowing the need for action? Analysis paralysis? (Hello, Enneagram 5 Quiet Specialist)

- Are you overwhelmed when simply asking for help or agreeing to a new timeline would relieve the pressure? Afraid to look weak or incompetent? (Hello, Enneagram 3 and 8 – Competitive Achiever/Active Controller)

TAKE CARE OF YOUR OWN BACK YARD BEFORE BEING THE WORLD'S SAVIOR.

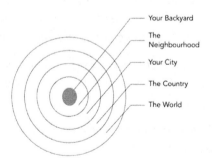

Spiritual teachers say that if you want to make the biggest difference in the world, fix yourself. Once that's done, move to your neighborhood … and so on.

How's your backyard? Is your organization's stuff handled? If not, you are in no position to be anyone else's savior. Oxygen mask on yourself first.

You will be surprised what a few weeks or months of focused effort will do to get your house in order. A conversation with your boss about the things you are addressing will go a long way in getting you breathing room.

MANAGING YOUR VISIONARY

Meeting with my client and their visionary CEO in four acts.

Mark: *"Dennis and I discussed his responsibility as being the number two to a visionary leader (you)."* She liked that. *"I told him it is his job to triage the staggering number of ideas and creativity coming from you. As the implementer to your visionary, he should never say no ..."*

CEO interrupts with a sheepish smile: *"He should never tell me no."* She regretted it as soon as she said it ... but she meant it.

Mark: *"Exactly, he should never say no. It is his job to take it all in, consider it and help you prioritize together. He knows the resources, workload on the team and often the downstream effects of many of your ideas. He needs clearly to help you understand that together you have an agreed upon plan to move forward."*

CEO: *"Yes, that's exactly what I need. A sounding board. I know I'm moving a million miles an hour. I don't want to stop but I need help getting focused."*

Dennis: *"How can I best make you aware of the impact of a project so you can hear it?"*

They then chose words to use and made an agreement on how to handle the pushback needed in the future.

There are many ways of pushing back without saying no. Of course, they may say, "Do it anyway." Even the best bosses will. Then it's time to FITFO – Figure It The F*$& Out.

If that happens too often, I see a feedback conversation in your future. This relationship is dynamic, you will need to consistently communicate and adjust so you are in alignment with their goals and manage them from making your job impossible.

ATTITUDE ADJUSTMENT

For your own survival, it is your job to focus your boss.

To help your boss focus, and to be able to push back effectively, you must know their ultimate goal and bring them back to it.

Remember the visionary/implementer relationship from the Wickman and Winters book.

For access to worksheets and other resources go to

https://bit.ly/46r8u8u

Leading Across

LEADING ON A TEAM OF PEERS

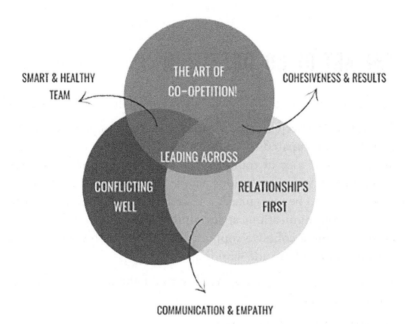

Chapter 4

THE ART OF CO-OPETITION

Podcast Interviewer: "Mark, what do you mean by "Leading Across?""

Mark, taking a deep breath, "Leading on a team of powerful leaders is next level compared to leading a team where you may have title, authority, and tons of training. The question is, how do you lead in a group of smart, ambitious people who have their own agenda, a need/want to be recognized, a vested interest in their ideas, fears, triggers, communications styles, unresolved playground issues, all while creating a cohesive supportive team that is one voice to the organization and outside world?"

Interviewer: "That's exhausting. I've never thought of it that way, but you are right."

Neither had I, until that moment.

If you have ever done any leadership training, I am sure you've been put in a room with a group of people with a problem or challenge to solve. Whether it's building a tower with just string and straws, solving an escape room, or presenting the best solution to a pretend issue, it is an intense experience.

Why is it intense? Because you are trying to figure out how to get the job done, be a team player, assert your ideas, not be an asshole, and win the freaking game with a bunch of people trying to do the same.

It is a powerful mirror of how you operate under pressure. Done right, you get to see your natural inclinations to take over or hang back, to be flexible or hurt when your idea is rejected. You get to lose gracefully or cast blame.

Welcome to leading across … in the real world.

"I'm a sports fanatic, so competition comes easy to me. But I think inside of an organization, competition doesn't necessarily mean you have winners and losers. As a competitor, I want to be able to set the example. I want to be able to develop best practices that other people can then adopt and be successful as well. I think you can be competitive, and also be focused on the greater good of the organization as well.

Microsoft, part of the evaluation criteria is, "What have you done to help other people in the business outside of your role or responsibility?" That was in every employee review.

A rising tide raises all boats, so that's how I look at competition from a peer perspective. Obviously, I want to be the shining star in the organization. I want my team to be the shining star. But at the end of the day, we want to make sure that the entire business and the people are improving."

Michael D. Robinson
The Rising Leader Podcast episode 23:
"Leadership, Authenticity, Accountability and Values"
https://bit.ly/3SUIe3p

My friend, Spiritual Teacher Teo Alfero runs a sanctuary for rescued wolves and wolfdogs called Wolf Connection in California. In Teo's book, *The Wolf Connection* he teaches how humans and wolves evolved alongside one another and that because of those interaction, humans have derived much of our social organization from wolf pack structure. One of the things I've learned is that yes, there is an alpha wolf breeding pair, but that wolves take turns leading, depending on the job at hand. The best hunter, not necessarily the alpha, leads the hunt. Whatever the pack needs, they pick the best wolf to lead that objective and the rest become good followers, including the alphas.

Good leaders need to be good followers.

Take a moment to reflect. How do you show up in a group dynamic?

How do you get your voice heard? Do you step to the front or hang back? If the group rejects your idea, do you settle in to being a good soldier?

Leading, without authority, on a team of other leaders is next level!

For this section, your team is the leadership team you share responsibilities with. In the next section, "your team" will be those you lead.

"The key to being a leader is to be able to follow first. Too many leaders have no idea how to follow, they only know how to tell people what to do. Especially if you're a type A personality. Then there are the people who think they are an "alpha" when in charge and a "beta" when they are not. That is also incorrect.

Do you think that a whole platoon of Navy SEALs going into a target are full of betas with only one alpha? No fucking way. Every one of those dudes is an alpha in their own way. They lead when they need to lead, and they follow when they need to follow. It's something that we teach in the SEAL team training. When it is your responsibility, you are in charge, I listen to you. When it's mine, I'm in charge. We have these very clear lanes, roles, and responsibilities.

Also, I can ask for help or ask someone to cover if I need. That doesn't take away my power or authority. And so that I can do the other thing that I need to do well, it doesn't take away my authority or my power when someone else comes in. I have to be okay with that.

It's like going into a building and clearing rooms. If I drop a threat area, I know that my buddy is going to come behind me and pick it up. Because that's the way that we were taught, that's the thing that we're supposed to do. If I'm out there leading, I might have to be holding security on something, and I have to wait for someone to come in. I can't just leave that responsibility, because a bad guy could pop out and smoke us all. That's not okay. I have to do that sort of lower-level responsibility until one of my guys comes in, and bumps me out so that I can start leading the train on that mission on that target again.

It's something that has to be taught, it has to be part of the culture of the organization. If you're not driving as a leader, if you're not driving the culture in your organization, then someone else is. And that's just the bottom line."

William Branum, Navy SEAL Veteran and
Founder Naked Warrior Recovery
The Rising Leader Podcast episode 52:
"The Navy SEAL Secrets to Leadership"
https://bit.ly/3vmuPY6

WHOSE TEAM ARE YOU ON?

I ask you, "Who is your team?" Well, that depends.

You lead a team as I pointed out above. They are the people in the organization you are responsible for. You work together for an objective, you support them, you fight alongside them, advocate for them, and protect them when you need to.

You work so closely with these people that you can easily fall into the trap of thinking that it is your primary team. You can easily fall into an "Us against Them dynamic."

ATTITUDE ADJUSTMENT

You are now "them."

Even though you are the captain of your ship and have an unshakable loyalty to your crew,
they are no longer your primary team.

Of course, it's not either/or … it's both/and – slightly weighted.

That means your team and loyalty is to the CEO, executive leadership team and the well-being of the company as a whole. This is your team.

"At the beginning of our careers we succeed and get promoted from the work we do individually. As we rise through the organization, it shifts from our contribution to the work of our team. We will be measured on leadership skills, our ability to succeed through others.

As we get more senior, our focus elevates further. While we are responsible for the success of the organization under us, we also need to shift to an enterprise perspective.

This track not only brings the changes in responsibility, impact and perspective, but comes with shifting sources of stress.

Your ability to succeed and thrive will correlate to your ability to address these new challenges."

Helen Appleby, author
The Unwritten Rules of Women's Leadership.

You can hear more from Helen on *The Rising Leader Podcast* episode 59 here: https://bit.ly/3SdMREU

Once you understand this your life and decisions will be clearer. You will be a better and more effective leader for the team that reports to you when you understand this dynamic.

Since is it is more of a balancing act than an either/or, let's look at it as "your center of gravity."

Let's say 60% Leadership Team/40% The Team that Reports to You. Does that help clarify?

Here is an example of a Coaching Agreement from an actual recent 360-feedback report.

Coaching Objective:	From a leader who:	To a leader who:
Executive Team	thinks only of their silo/ department/team	knows they are on the Executive Leadership Team first, and thinks of the global organization.

The CEO and several members of the leadership team offer feedback for John, the Chief Marketing Officer of a global tech company, that he is more protective of his team than the company.

The people in his organization oversee advertising, brand alliances, subject matter experts (brand evangelists), marketing statistics, web techs and social media managers. He is very protective of his team, the budget, and how their effectiveness is seen.

He's great at his job. And, the consistent feedback from the executive team members I interviewed was that he is more combative and competitive rather than cooperative. The words they used in the 360 interviews were "me-focused" and "my team focused." It was a value of the CEO that his leadership team be a tight-knit group that work together.

When he heard the criticism, John pushed back. "Marketing takes a back seat to sales and product development in credit for success, budget, resources, and mostly in the CEOs eyes." John had a chip on his shoulder and wore his protectiveness of his organization as a badge of honor. He really did feel it was "us against them."

Rationale aside, his attitude caused disruption and distrust on the leadership team. He also had a bad habit of coming out of leadership team meetings and saying things like, "Well I fought for you" or "They are going in this direction — we are screwed again." Once John understood the impact of his words on his team, he saw what he was doing. The victim language and posture he used had the opposite effect on the people that counted on him. He is mature and committed to his own development so when he saw how he was showing up in black and white, he was mortified and committed to the adjustments. Within two months, he was back to "Trusted Advisor" status AND a more effective advocate for his organization.

Can you see yourself in any of this?

Can you find evidence for your organization feeling like the forgotten child at the table? Or maybe one of the other exec's doesn't work as hard as you but gets more credit. Remember, the ego is a powerful thing. John fell into the trap of resentment which created behaviors that didn't match his values. It happens to all of us.

Remember the center of gravity, you can fight like hell behind closed doors, but once you walk out of the leadership team meeting, you speak with one voice.

Being a leader of your team, however difficult, is infinitely simpler than being a leader amongst leaders. This is where you leave your ego at the door, put yourself in the CEOs seat and learn to think globally, act accordingly.

You are now playing soccer or basketball, not golf. Passing and strategy are more important for the win than your superstar talents. And you still get to make winning goals.

Michael Jordan, arguably the best basketball player that ever lived (my book, my opinion), did not win a championship in his first eight seasons as a Chicago Bull, even when he was the top scorer in the NBA.

His problem? He was the star, and didn't trust his team. It had to be him. It wasn't until he was on the 1992 Dream Team in the Olympics and was surrounded by the best of the best that he learn real leadership. He learned that others had skills he didn't have. He learned to trust them and work together for the win.

When Jordan returned to the NBA, he brought that new-found maturity with him. It was only then that we saw he and the Bulls win ring after ring. They did it as a team, and I still remember nights when it was a Michael Jordan Fireworks show.

Things to keep in mind when you are on a championship team.

- There are stars on every team, and the team needs to support them, but to be successful at a championship level, the stars need to support the team
- Everyone brings something to the table, you are better together
- You get to have your ambition, but not at the cost of the health of the team.
- Switch to a truly Win Win Win attitude.

You are the voice of the company now:

It's easy to use leaky language with the people you are in the trenches with every day. It's almost natural to fall into us versus them … forgetting you are "them."

Catch yourself.

Move From This	To This
"I fought for you in the leadership meeting but I just wasn't able to get it through."	"We've decided that you are not going to get that promotion right now."

> "I didn't agree with their decision, but that's the way they want to go."

> "We talked it through, and we are not going in that direction at this time."

You can no longer be "Good Cop" to the leadership team's "Bad Cop."

Let's Reflect

- What situations have come up where you felt you had to balance the needs of your team and those of the leadership team/CEO? How did you handle it?
- Think of a time when you disagreed with the leadership team's decision. How did you communicate this to your team and the people involved?
- Whose team were you on?
- Did treating it the way you did truly serve the person/ people or did it just make you feel better?
- With this new perspective, how could you handle it better next time? How will you adjust your communications to present a unified front with the leadership team?

INNER HURDLES THAT GET IN THE WAY

Every time you move up the ladder, the drunk monkeys start their circus in your head. It is different for everyone, but these are the common inner hurdles I have to clear with fast-rising leaders. If they fester, they manifest as bad behavior on your leadership team. Check if any of these resonate with you.

Peer group whiplash – Managing people you used to work with. This often shows up as managing through affability. You are trying to straddle the fence of boss and friend. You will need to let go of that; it muddies the water and ends up doing more damage than intended.

If you have "friends" on the team, have a heart to heart with them. Establish work and personal guidelines to keep the relationship clean.

Wealth and Privilege Guilt – I run into this especially when someone comes from humble beginnings. Embracing your position of authority and the social standing that comes with it can feel like a betrayal. Watch this attitude. Humility is not the same as guilt. Learn to own what you've earned (the monkeys may say differently), and humility will come faster.

Entitlement – Leadership is a humbling experience. People don't work for you, they work for themselves. You lead them in the work the company needs them to accomplish. Every great leader I have met feels they have the privilege of working for their team, and by helping them get what they need to be successful.

Invisible Responsibilities versus Visible Work – Your job is no longer to do the work, it is to make sure the right work gets done. The better your team runs, the less you will have to "do." Strategy, leading, coaching, and problem-solving can feel less productive than actually completing a project. Learn to get your satisfaction from seeing your team succeed.

Imposter Syndrome – Do we really need to discuss this? If you've been promoted, you've never done this job before. You are learning on the job. We are all figuring it out as we go, the drunk monkeys love to have a field day with this one. Contrary to the monkey's insistence, they didn't make a mistake when they gave you the position.

Delegation Hesitation – So many monkey mind reasons not to delegate. We will cover them in Leading Your Team. The less you properly delegate, the more overwhelmed you will be, the less effective your team will be. Overwhelm will impact your behavior and comfort on the leadership team.

Any combination of the above is garden variety head trash for successful people. Talk with someone you trust, journal, but don't hide from it. Your humanity will make you a better leader.

"Anything that's different than what you would expect from the survival mentality, is completely opposite of what it expects, so naturally the survivor self is going to have an objection to that. And that's why we're scared. But the scared is not really the real us. The real us recognizes reality. That's the conflict. That's the battle. So when we recognize, "Oh, yeah, well, that's my survivor self trying to talk me out of the champion's secret mindset or creating a life of value and full potential, then it makes sense. If we don't understand this biology, and we identify with the survivor as us, rather than a biology that is there to protect us, then you're always going to be in doubt about what you believe about yourself.

That's why understanding this duality of how we're constructed from a biological standpoint is absolutely essential, because you can't shut it off. But if you recognize, hey, that's the imposter me, That's the real imposter syndrome. The real impostor syndrome is that we believe that this is the real self and the real us is not our potential."

Dr. Jeff Spencer, coach to elite performers
The Rising Leader Podcast episode 37:
"Playing the Bigger Game"
https://bit.ly/3QVeCQL

CHECKING YOUR AMBITION

Let's talk about your ambition — that drive for success that got you here. You are reading this book *because* you are a fast-rising leader, a high achiever that outshone everyone else to get promoted. It worked … brilliantly.

Some of us have outworked everyone to get where we are. Others among us have been affable and likeable while we got promoted and stay that way even though that skill is holding us back now.

Some of us have stepped on some toes, maybe even been a little cutthroat. Even the most well intentioned of us cause a little wreckage with our ambition and immaturity.

A conversation I have had with a new "bull-in-a-china-shop" type client:

"You have a choice. Do you want to be the leader who people resent? One where they talk behind your back saying you throw people under the bus for your gain, and didn't deserve the promotion? Or do you want to be the person who everyone points to and says, "Yes, she totally deserved the position. I'd follow her anywhere." It's your choice."

Which are you?

Let's Reflect

Can you think of a time when your ambition was at the expense of someone else?

What was the consequence to them?

What was the consequence to you? Did you lose an ally?

Of course, sometimes someone must lose for someone to win. But it's the how that determines the nature of that game.

On your way up, have you built a bench of supporters who have your back? Or did you cause some damage along the way so you always feel someone is gunning for you?

The most successful leaders are the ones who everyone is thrilled for when they get the promotion (even if they personally wanted that job).

REPAIRING THE WRECKAGE OF YOUR AMBITION

"I was able to make sure that my team and my work was recognized by senior management, and that they understood the value and contributions we were making to the organization. People saw that and would come to me and ask for advice on how to handle particular situations. In that environment, I became the therapist for a number of those team members. It's something that I enjoyed doing, and I still enjoy it to this day, I also enjoy helping people see their strengths. Part of that is to be able to be authentic and honest about your observations of other team members, whether they be subordinates or peers, or even, speaking truth to management. I've never been shy.

You have to have a passion for people or you're not going to be very successful. It is about coaching, mentoring, understanding what motivates other people, and it's also about helping people through tough times in their career and address challenges they are experiencing."

Michael D. Robinson
The Rising Leader Podcast episode 23:
"Authenticity, Accountability and Values"
https://bit.ly/3SUIe3p

Let's take a look back on your career together, shall we?

Make a list of people you know you did wrong intentionally, or unintentionally. You will want to justify, but resist the urge. And you may not have crossed anyone. Go over your history and scan the names and faces. Pause on the ones you don't feel right about in your gut. If someone comes to mind again, your mind will want to gloss over and explain it away. "It wasn't so bad."

Making amends, even for the smallest things, is a potent relationship builder.

Get clear on what happened and what your responsibility in the situation was. Take 100% responsibility. Time to go back and make amends like an alcoholic on the 8th and 9th steps in AA.

8 – *Made a list of all persons we had harmed and became willing to make amends to them all.*

9- *Made direct amends to such people wherever possible, except when to do so would injure them or others.*

I promise you will feel unburdened. You may be received with a satisfactory forgiveness, you may not. That is not your concern, your concern is just doing it.

Always remember, use your own words, they will ring truer than mine. And, here are a few examples.

- I understand that I treated you this way or handled this situation in this manner.
- It was wrong (careful of justification).
- I am learning to be better and I apologize.
- It will be different going forward.
- If not, you have my permission to bring it to my attention.

This is one of the most profound actions a person can take. Often, trust can be built back better than it was originally when we take responsibility, and actually shift our behavior going forward.

Sometimes you need to do this in real time (we are human after all).

Anne, Joe and Dave are director level leaders in a manufacturing firm. They are colleagues and friends outside of work. Joe is talented and smart but struggling to lead his team. Leadership is newer to him and he lacks skills communicating direction and giving feedback to his team. His team have been known to complain about it to Anne and Dave. Anne and Dave truly support and love Joe, they are good friends ... and they are human. The three were working on a project together. On an email that was meant to be just between Anne and Dave, Dave makes an offhanded comment about the complaints of Joe's team, and Anne responded immediately with a comment about how it affects her team negatively.

You see where this is going? They copied Joe unintentionally. The damage was done.

I coach Dave so he called me immediately. He told me the story, then ...

"I'm going to tell him that I didn't really mean it and that he is a good leader."

"But you did mean it?"

"Yes, but I can't say that ... it'll hurt his feelings."

"Too late. What was going on with you that you felt comfortable gossiping about your friend and colleague?"

After a bit of reflecting and coaching, "I was frustrated that his people were coming to me, and if I'm honest, it made me feel better about myself to be one up. Shit, that's ugly."

Ego is always ugly.

"What should you have done, Dave?"

"I should have gone directly to him with the feedback."

"And?"

"And shared my own leadership challenges and offered to help."

"Now what?"

"I'm going to go to him, and apologize. Admit to being petty, share my own insecurities and challenges, and offer to work on this together."

He had the conversation. Joe listened, admitted to feeling betrayed by both he and Anne. It took a few days, and a night out having a beer, but eventually, with candor and heart, the relationship was repaired with a new level of trust.

Confront it immediately. Be honest and humble. Commit to being better.

As a general rule, the longer you take to address an issue, the bigger it becomes.

If you confront it in the moment, it's no big deal.

Go back quickly, it's a little more serious.

Wait too long and say, "we need to have a talk." Now it's a thing.

"Too often, leaders are hesitant to admit they made a mistake, or to apologize, because they think it makes them look weaker when, in fact, it's the opposite. If they could just understand how much people appreciate and are relieved when they hear somebody say, I'm sorry, or I apologize for saying that or doing that in the meeting. I had no idea it had that impact on you. I am committed to being different. You have my permission to hold me accountable and asking to be held accountable. That creates trust and psychological safety."

Meredith Bell, President and Cofounder
Tools For Strengthing Communication Skills
The Rising Leader Podcast episode 3:
"Growing Strong Leaders Through a Culture of Coaching"
https://bit.ly/3GfVtnG

LEADING FROM WITHIN

Confidence plus Enrollment Skills is the key to success in leading on a team of leaders.

We discussed self-worth and confidence in Speaking your Mind, but I want to revisit it here.

Make sure you are supported outside of and inside the work environment so you can be your best when needed.

Having a coach, mentor, or group of friends you can bring your doubts and insecurities to will be immensely helpful. I would never write a book, get on a stage, or confront a CEO if I didn't have my "posse" who have my back.

My clients and I roleplay and rehearse important conversations frequently.

- Lack of confidence and self-worth will sabotage your leadership.
- Most of us have challenges to our self-worth. Recognize and acknowledge it, bring it to your support team, so you do not act from it.

- Your feelings are valid, and we will learn more how to work with them in Leading You.

THE RULES OF CO-OPETITION

- There are so many competing things going on at once that learning skills to lead at this level is key.
- Resist the urge to shine at the expense of others.
- Win allies rather than creating competitors.
- Be so good you can't be ignored and as a result stand out.

For access to worksheets and other resources go to
https://bit.ly/46r8u8u

Chapter 5

CONFLICTING WELL

"A leadership team is a small group of people who are collectively responsible for achieving a common objective for their organization."

~ Patrick Lencioni

In his book *The Five Dysfunctions of a Team* author Patrick Lencioni teases out some very useful attributes that contribute to a team's success.

We all know that for an organization to succeed, there must be a strategy to execute on, effective marketing and sales, a sound financial model, and something valuable to deliver - a technology. He calls this a Smart Team.

Then there is the people side.

Leaders, Marketing People, Finance People, Sales People, Technical People. All come with personality traits, agendas, and humanity.

A company that keeps politics to a minimum, communicates with clarity, has high morale and productivity, and can keep turnover low, is deemed a "Healthy Team."

"Sometimes good people have tantrums. There was a situation where one of my vice presidents and the head of one of my business units had come to a massive head. He sent me a scathing email, "We can't work together; I'm going to quit etc." I said to the VP, "You're an adult, I want you to go back and read the email that you sent to me. Once you've read it, call me back. He called me back and said, "I'm embarrassed."

"I said, you should be embarrassed. Here's the reality. You can work here, or you cannot work here. If you can't figure this out, we're going have to make a change."

I heard nothing more from either of them.

A year later I asked, "Hey, how are things going with _____?"

"Man, it's going fricking awesome. I can't believe all the friction is out of the gears."

John Sapone, Senior Vice President of Sale, Snowflake
The Rising Leader Podcast episode 16:
"The Making of a Sales Leader"
https://bit.ly/47yVjE6

I've adapted some of Patrick Lencioni's work over time into the talks and workshops that I give. I feel it is important to note that I admire his work immensely and lean on it in the following …

THE GOAL: A SMART AND HEALTHY TEAM

WHAT IS A SMART AND HEALTHY TEAM?

- Strategy
- Marketing
- Finance
- Technology

- Minimal Politics
- Minimal Confusion
- High Morale
- High Productivity
- Low Turnover

Which do you think is more important to the success of the company. Smart or healthy?

I do know some smart companies with great products that are toxic to work for, yet are successful. They have so much demand that they can ignore (for now) so they are not the norm.

Lencioni agrees: "A smart, unhealthy team is doomed to failure, but a healthy team that is not so smart can succeed. People working together can overcome incredible obstacles … and eventually become smart."

How do you know if your team is healthy?

Lencioni explains that it is a hierarchy resembling the adapted illustration below.

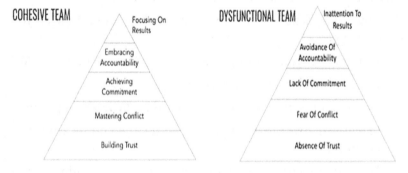

Source: *The Five Dysfunctions of a Team,* Patrick Lencioni

Let's Reflect

For now, focus on the leadership team. Later apply the same thought process to the team you lead in the organization. Rate each on a scale of 1 to 5:

	My Team	Leadership Team
• Trust:		
• Conflict		
• Commitment		
• Accountability		
• Results		

When you look at the highest and lowest scores, what do you think?

Remember, you cannot manage conflict well if you do not have trust. There is no accountability without commitment. Results are a result of the entire pyramid being intact. Your job is to find the challenge closest to the base and work on that first.

Once you identify where the team needs to work, how do you effect change?

Gandhi's got you: "Be the change you wish to see in the world."

It starts by asking the right questions.

"How can I be the change I want to see in the leadership team?"

"How can I set the example and foster the culture I want in my organization?"

You can influence a lot by being an example and holding others to that standard.

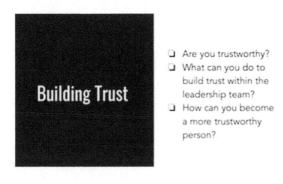

Building Trust

❑ Are you trustworthy?
❑ What can you do to build trust within the leadership team?
❑ How can you become a more trustworthy person?

Mastering Conflict

- ❏ How do you deal with conflict?
- ❏ What can you do to conflict better with your peers?
- ❏ Coming up: Conflicting Well.

Achieving Commitment

- ❏ Do you try to get buy-in from your peers?
- ❏ Do you stick to the decisions you collectively make as a team?
- ❏ Do you ask for clarity around what you are trying to achieve?

Achieving Commitment

- ❏ Are you rowing in the same direction as the rest of the Leadership Team?
- ❏ How can you improve commitment within the Leadership Team?

Embracing Accountability	❏ Do you say what you are going to do and do what you are going to say? ❏ Do you communicate when you are not going to keep an agreement?
Embracing Accountability	❏ Are you focussed on creating strong agreements vs. setting expectations?
Focusing On Results	❏ Is the objective clear? ❏ Do you execute? ❏ Do you achieve the stated goals of your organization?

Don't try to boil the ocean. What specifically does your organization (your leadership team) need to focus on in order to be smart and healthy? Remember, focus on the base of the pyramid. Get that solid, the next will follow more easily.

OVERCOMMUNICATE TO BUILD BETTER RELATIONSHIPS

I spend 90% of my time teaching and coaching through difficult conversations. Just as a married couple stand a better chance of making it if they fight well and fair, so does a team. With the pressure and responsibility that you carry as a leader of an organization, you will bump heads. Your ambitions may not align, mistakes get made. If you trust each other, and can work to resolution, your odds of sustainable success go way up.

> **RELATIONSHIPS ARE MADE AND BROKEN IN BOTH THE COMMUNICATED AND UNCOMMUNICATED.**
>
> **BY WHAT YOU SAY, AND WHAT YOU DON'T SAY.**

- Business Communications
  - Agreement of work product, quality, timing
  - Feedback, vision, priorities
  - Responsibilities, workload, credit

    - Who is responsible for the result, who is actually doing the work and who gets the credit for it.

- Non-business Communications
  - Have I stepped on your toes?
  - Have I dropped something out?
  - Did I not do something you asked me to do?
  - Did I hurt our feelings?
  - Did I not praise you or your work enough?

We are talking all the touchy feely stuff we hate to talk about at work.

HINT: IT'S ALL REAL EVEN IF WE DON'T TALK ABOUT IT. MIGHT AS WELL TALK ABOUT IT, RIGHT?

Where do you need to over-communicate?

Business Communication: Status, responsibility, Vision. Quality, Timeline, Compensation (Dashboards are your friend)

Non-business Communications are trickier and where most of the challenges occur.

Keep in mind:

- Trust your gut.
- Schedule time to check in with people:
- How are we doing?
- I've been heads down doing my own thing; how is our relationship?
- If you feel something if off; check it out.
- Hone your spidey senses.

Your paranoia is welcome. It will feel silly; speak up anyway.

Let's say everyone is going to Top Golf for a night of drinks and fun. You didn't get invited.

What is your pattern of reaction when something like this happens? Do you sulk quietly and wonder what is wrong with you? Do you nurture resentment and create rivalries in the office, complaining to anyone who will listen? Or do you assume that a mistake was made and show up confidently and hit the ball and buy some drinks?

Be honest as you reflect. The challenge with relationships is that we bring our patterns, conditioning, hurts, and histories to every situation. If you were popular as a kid, you probably aren't phased by the invitation oversight. If you were picked last for sports, this may hurt more than it should.

We are all five-year-olds who shave or put on makeup.

We need to honor and understand that in ourselves. Honor and speak to it in others.

It's not rational or professional. It's almost always invisible or masked by other behavior.

But that 5-year-old is always there.

Trusting yourself and overcommunicating will help keep the pipes of relationship clear and flowing. It starts with you.

You walk out of a meeting and you get a passing sense that you railroaded someone in the meeting. Easy to explain it away as no big deal and say nothing. That is a missed opportunity.

Go find out ... build relationship.

"Hey, in the meeting I felt like I talked over you."

The answer will be either, "No, I didn't feel that way at all," to which you create more trust by saying, "Great, thanks. If I ever do, please let me know. It's not my intention." Or the response will be, "Yes, and it was rude. You do that a lot." Now you have created more trust by acknowledging the behavior and working through the amends and solution going forward.

Hint: it may have been true in the first scenario but they didn't want to speak up. You still created trust, because they will be able to address it next time.

Let's Reflect

Scan your team in your mind. Does your attention go to any particular person, situation or conversation? There may or may not be something there. Go find out anyway.

SIX TYPES OF DIFFICULT CONVERSATIONS

1. Boundary Management – saying no
2. Giving Feedback – accountability
3. Asking or Help – clarification
4. Delegating
5. Creating Agreements
6. Renegotiating

SAYING NO AND SETTING BOUNDARIES

No is a complete sentence. Successful people say yes to everything, super successful people say no to almost everything … creating the ability to focus on the truly important.

It takes courage to say no. All the internal voices (I'll look overwhelmed, they won't like me) will run wild. The consequences of saying no may even be true. The way to deal with that is to be exceptional at what you do, show up in a big way when people really need support, and respect other people's boundaries.

Still, while no might be the best answer, it might not be the right word, especially when talking with your boss. Sometimes an outright "no" is too harsh or could even be inappropriate. What we need is to take a beat, and break free from the automatic reaction in order to know the more constructive response. You need a moment to be able to respond in the manner that best supports the situation.

Take a deep breath.

Use reflective listening if you need more than a moment.

Remember earlier we used the phrase, "Yes, I could take this on, and … ?"

The "and" brings the asker into the prioritization process. You can also negotiate, "Yes, I will do this for you, but I need in order to be able to accommodate your request."

This is a great way to negotiate your time and attention in a way that works for you.

"May I get back to you," is one of the most effective sentences I have ever learned for getting between me and an automatic yes. You can get back to the person in 5 minutes or the next day. You give yourself the opportunity to get some perspective. The trick is to eliminate the automatic "Yes" that you may regret later and take control of your resources.

Remember, you *cannot* fail.

BOUNDARIES

Good fences make great neighbors. Clear boundaries make for great relationships. Boundaries are the antidote to resentments.

In my workshops I assert, "If I have a resentment, it is because I haven't set a boundary, asked for what I want/need, or I am just a bit jealous." After some back and forth, I can usually get the participants to see the victimhood in resentment. Most think of setting boundaries as an offensive or aggressive action. I see it as an authentic relationship conversation.

If you understand yourself, what you need to perform at your best, what your values are, and are clear what work needs to be done so you can be most effective, you will at least know which boundaries are important.

There are non-negotiable boundaries and negotiable. Get clear on the few things you must have and communicate them … clearly.

The rest is where you negotiate.

"I have breakfast with my family every day. This is non-negotiable for me. However, I will stay late when needed, and on the days that my presence is essential, I will skip that breakfast."

I do not speak to clients before 8:30 am because in order to show up the way I want to show up, I must have my meditation, journaling, and exercise time in the morning. It is non-negotiable. And there are days, when my clients have been in crisis, where I have taken calls on my elliptical. Those are the exception.

You may be sheepish at first, apologizing and explaining while setting and enforcing a boundary and that's okay. You will get better and clearer with practice. Once you see that people, for the most part, will respect your boundaries, especially if you are flexible where you can be, it becomes easier. You will be more effective, helpful, and more authentic in your relationships as you learn this skill.

FEEDBACK

The willingness and ability to give good honest feedback is probably the most important skill a leader can have and also the most difficult to master. Let's hear directly from Kim Scott from our discussion on *The Rising Leader Podcast*.

"There is an order of operations to creating a culture of feedback. The first step in the order of operations is to solicit feedback, don't dish it out. Prove that you can take it. If you can create an organization in which people know that you genuinely want to hear when you're screwing up, and that you will reward them for telling you, and that you will either fix the problem, or you will you will explain to them why you disagree in a respectful way, you are on your way.

There are four things to keep in mind when you solicit feedback. By the way, the best moment to solicit feedback is at the end of every one on one or the last five minutes of a meeting.

Step number two is to make sure you are giving consistent and specific praise.

The best feedback I've ever gotten in my career has always happened in these impromptu two-minute conversations. You don't want to save it up for your one-on-one meeting, and you definitely don't want to save it up for a performance review. You want to make sure that you're thinking very clearly about giving it in the moment. Of course, everything I'm saying has exceptions. If the other person is super upset, then wait, until a better moment.

You also want to praise in public criticize in private. You want to make sure that your praise is specific and sincere, and that your criticism is kind and clear.

Radical candor is what happens when you care personally and [are] challenged directly at the same time. It's useful to think about what radical candor is not. Sometimes we remember to challenge directly, but we forgot to show that we care personally. And that I call obnoxious aggression, you can imagine a two-by-two graph. The vertical line is care personally and the horizontal line is challenged directly. Upper right hand quadrant is radical candor, bottom right hand quadrant is obnoxious aggression. In an earlier version of the book, I call that the asshole quadrant, because it seemed clearer. I stopped doing that, because I found that when I did, people would use this framework to start writing names in boxes. I beg of you, don't use this framework that way.

ON AUTHENTIC VERSUS OBNOXIOUS

Very often when we talk about being authentic, people confuse that for meaning they can do or say whatever they want. That it's irrelevant how it lands on the other person. They are the so called truth tellers. That is not authenticity, that's just obnoxious aggression.

Use Radical candor as a framework, like a compass, to guide specific conversations with specific people to a better place.

For example, if the other person is sad or mad, move up on the care personally dimension.

Or, sometimes a person will just brush you off. You've worked up your courage to say the thing, and they just don't hear you. You then need to go further out on the challenge directly dimension, then you may be comfortable going.

You have to pay attention to what's going on for the other person."

Kim Scott, author *Radical Candor*
The Rising Leader Podcast episode 25:
"The Art of Radical Candor"
https://bit.ly/3RgOO2T

We are seeking balance.

Some general guidelines for effective feedback.

- You go first – ask for, listen to, and act on feedback.
- Address quickly, the longer you wait the heavier the conversation.
- Positive feedback – is feedback,
- What went well – even better if.
- Use specifics.
  - This observable thing happened
  - The impact of this thing is
  - What this needs to look like is
- Be curious.

Like boundaries, giving feedback is a practice that gets better with regular use.

ASKING FOR HELP OR CLARITY

Of course, if you can find the answer yourself, do it. Show some initiative. I have a friend who says, "If you can Google it, don't ask me." But if you are having difficulty, consider how much spinning your wheels unnecessarily costs you. I've heard all the excuses: I don't want to look dumb or lazy, I pride myself on being a self-starter, I don't want to bother anyone, and they are busy too.

This is where your commitment to the project is more important than saving face. If you cannot figure it out on your own, (or with ChatGPT), or it is just going to take valuable time away from the project, you need to ask for help. Remember it's not about you, it's about the project.

If you need help, resources, training, or more time ... ask. They can say no. Then you can decide if you want to go to bat for your ask or find another way. If the "they" in this scenario are equally committed to the project and have respect for you, they will work on a solution. It may be a simple as someone has more experience and they can take ten minutes to save you and the project four hours. If you were the "they" wouldn't you want four hours saved if it could be done?

If you don't understand something ... get clear. Clarity is your responsibility. You will save yourself and everyone else numerous iterations from the start.

DELEGATING AND SUCCESS THROUGH OTHERS

"As you get more senior, your job is less and less to do the work and more and more to make sure the right work gets done, so you can focus on the things only you can do."

~ Helen Appleby

The way to make sure the right work gets done is to delegate and empower. Delegate and coach. Delegate and teach.

There are so many excuses for not delegating.

- The team is already too busy.
- They won't do it as well as I can.
- I'll just have to redo it.
- It's quicker to do it myself.
- I like doing it.
- Fear of being irrelevant.

I have had more than one client, who learned effective delegation, express, "I have all this free time. I don't even know what my job is anymore."

Sounds crazy, doesn't it? But it's normal. If you are used to being a high achiever working your way through a pile of work, and now you are leading a team to do exponentially what you had done, you may not "feel" the satisfaction of doing it yourself. You will need to get that satisfaction from seeing the results of the team. You are now free to focus on the strategic parts of your job, which you complained you didn't have time for before.

Every step up the ladder, your responsibility increases, and you have less control. As you climb the ladder your contribution becomes increasingly strategic.

Every step up you need to let go of something tactical that you did well and maybe even enjoyed.

Every step up you will feel less and less like you DO anything. Hint: the best leaders are never "busy."

Every step up your job will become more people focused.

Every step up you will need to sharpen your coaching skills.

Success through others means giving your team the tough, challenging, work.

It means critiquing that work when it comes back ... both the awesome, and the not-so- awesome.

It means doing the above over and over until that person learns what they need to learn so the work is done to the standard you set. It means, if you do any part of their work, you are selling them short.

Delegation, coaching, and empowerment are the base line mechanics of moving you to that strategic leadership.

CREATING STRONG AGREEMENTS

We all walk around frustrated with unmet "expectations." We expect people to act a certain way, get something done, use directionals when they change lanes, and make our mocha chai soy latte correctly. We expect things of our employees, spouses, kids, and bosses. Unfortunately, we walk around in a state of constant disappointment. Resentment. The godfather of coaching, Steve Chandler says,

"When you have an expectation, the best you can hope for is to come out even. You expect something and they do it. More often than not, they don't, so you are let down. If you drop all expectations, you spend your day delighted and surprised."

How do you feel and act when someone has an expectation of you? Human nature is to balk at pressure that is *put on us from someone else*. It is even more fun when the expectation was never verbalized, and you only found out afterwards.

Suffice to say, there is a better way. Create strong, clear, communicated agreements. I know I am more enthusiastic about a task or responsibility when I am involved in the creation of it. It takes extra time and effort ... and it is the best way to neutralize a future resentment or misunderstanding.

Expectations Vs. Agreements

Expectations	Agreements
• Often uncommunicated	• Creative
• Complaints = unmet expectations	• Relationship and co-authored
• Naturally rebellious	• Productive
• Disappointed or neutral outcome	• Communicates the gap
• Leads to frustration	• Basis for future negotiation
• Cowardly or lazy	• Courageous

This works in our personal lives as well. How often have you been angry at your partner because "they should know?" Has your teenager ever lived up to your expectation? My kids had written agreements, *that they signed*, so the "alternative facts" of any given conversation could not be in dispute. And this was when they were teenagers. They could be expected to break agreements ... but we had a tool for teaching and parenting.

I promise you, the more expectations you drop ... the happier you will be. The next time you send out a note saying roughly, "I want this done, and I want it done by Friday," expecting it to be done, try this in writing or preferably in a conversation.

"I'd like this done and we need it to be done by Friday. Is this possible?"

"No, we have three projects that are also due by Friday (that you also said were urgent) and we do not have the staff to fill the fourth."

"Shoot, what do we need to do to make sure this is done? It *is* urgent."

"Tell me which of the other projects can be pushed, approve overtime for five people, or get me three more people from another department for a few days."

"Got it, I'll let you know how to proceed." Now, Friday comes and we are all on the same page.

RENEGOTIATIONS

Renegotiation is an incredible tool. When an agreement deadline is coming up fast, and it's clear the objective will not be met ... that is the time to pick up the phone. Burying our head in the sand is not a proactive strategy. By doing this you will:

- Let the person counting on the deadline know in plenty of time what is going to happen or not happen.

- Create trust and relationship.

- Relieve pressure on yourself and your team from the unrealistic goal

- Probably come up with a creative way to an acceptable solution

Not keeping an agreement is unacceptable. But that doesn't mean you are in jail. Circumstances change. If you know you take agreements seriously, and that your word can be trusted, but something has changed to influence the situation, revisiting an agreement to keep it workable, is a difficult conversation that will benefit all concerned.

HOW AND WHEN TO SPEAK UP

I use my own life, state of mind, and emotions as a laboratory. Once I learned that nothing, absolutely nothing, is happening "out there," the work to unravel my own jail cell could begin. And I found that the answer to almost any problem was to speak up or take an action. Communication is a miracle. It brings the unseen to light. Not always, but often enough to improve most situations. If I consider someone's motivation is X, and that motivation (real or created in my mind) angers me, I can ask and find out if it *is* X or something completely different. Nine times out of ten, it is something completely different and reasonable.

Action is another key to the cell block door. Often the feeling that our tires are stuck in mud is nothing more than our own thinking. By taking action, no matter how small or even right, we get ourselves out of the ditch and to higher ground.

So how do I know when to speak up or what to say when I do?

Let's play.

Speak up

Challenge	Possible Conversation
▪ Resentment?	▪ Boundary/Jealousy
▪ Overwhelm?	▪ Delegate, ask for...
▪ Can't say no?	▪ May I get back to you?
▪ Unmet expectation?	▪ Create an agreement
▪ Want something?	▪ Ask
▪ Didn't understand?	▪ Get clarification
▪ Fear?	▪ 5-4-3-2-1/Ask for support

HOW TO KNOW YOU NEED TO HAVE A DIFFICULT CONVERSATION OR TAKE AN ACTION

For this experiment, I use a feeling or a thought as a trigger for communication or action.

RESENTMENT

If I feel a resentment, it is my cue that one of three things is going on:

1. I need to set a boundary.

2. I need to ask for something I want, or

3. I'm just jealous, such as jealous of their commitment and I need to look at the whole person or situation.

Go past the initial anger and justification for a moment. You may need to journal or take a walk to let the "feelings" subside.

See if you can find a way to see your part in the situation and what you may be able to do differently.

You will find yourself back in the driver's seat with more power to influence your situation.

OVERWHELM

Overwhelm is about catastrophizing the future. It is bringing the consequences of not getting something done by some arbitrary or real deadline, into the present moment. This is where some deep belly breaths and clarity becomes essential. I cannot tell you how many times I have walked a client through a to-do list and it ends up almost empty, but they just couldn't see it for themselves. Left to their own evaluation, everything has to get done, and get done now.

Look at each thing that is overwhelming you with a skeptical eye.

Does it need to be done by me, by me now, or even at all. Should it be delegated? Do I need help? Do I just need to renegotiate the deadline?

Remember: Speaking up, for example, asking for help or renegotiating a deadline could mean "I'm not good enough" to your internal heckler. Walking past him or her is the actual breakthrough.

More on this in Leading You as we go over the Only 10s methodology later.

SAYING NO

We've beat this one to death.

"May I get back to you," is the pause you need when you have trouble saying no.

UNMET EXPECTATION?

Expectations are ridiculous and kill relationships. If I have an expectation of someone and they do not live up to that uncommunicated bar I have set for them, again, it can be a trigger for me. Crap, did I not have a conversation and create an agreement with that person? Were they clear on instructions, timeframe, quality of work? Did they verbally reflect what they understood to be the resulting action? If not, as a leader, as a friend, as a parent, as a partner, it's on me.

WANT SOMETHING?

This is "Sales 101". Did I even ask for the sale? Of course, I'm being flippant, but damn, if that wasn't almost impossible for me to do. I'd have expectations, sure. Not communicated, not agreed upon, nothing ... so the result? I felt resentment. I could probably draw some fancy matrix to show how this is all a web of confusion that creates the jail cell, but I think you get the picture. The practice here ... get past that heckler and utter the words, "Would you be willing to ... or I want ..." Be prepared for a no (and a yes, which can be painful to the heckler – more later on that). We need to allow the no. Then, if it is important, Sales 102 is, get willing to enroll.

DIDN'T UNDERSTAND?

Asking for clarity is another tough one on the ego. It is also one of the biggest causes of procrastination in me and in people I lead. YouTube has been a revelation. There is a reason it is the number two search engine (and why Google bought it). I can learn what the noise is in my washer, how to change a sim card in an iPhone, or create a dot art mandala. Same at work or home. Asking for clearer instructions, asking someone with more experience to show us something, will make the project go faster and be done better.

Let's Reflect

Go back over your week.

- Was there a conversation or situation where speaking up might have changed the game?

- Is there a challenge you have that you would like to address? Use the Difficult Conversations worksheet to walk through the solution.

POLITICS

ATTITUDE ADJUSTMENT

It's not politics, it's enrollment.

"I hate playing politics," says every client I've ever had.

I do to. And I don't. You shouldn't either. Most people use politics as a way of shortcutting the real work. They feel they need to "suck up," curry favor, be seen, get credit to get ahead. This all comes from fear. You and I no longer come from fear in our behavior. We are not victims of who's in and who's out. We create our own path.

The first step is to realize, as we have discussed before, that your job is sales. You sell you. You sell your ideas. You create influence rather than resort to politics.

I just got back from a talk by Victor Hoskins, The President and CEO of the Fairfax County Economic Authority. Victor was animated, funny, passionate, insightful, and very, very talkative. He owned the room. He said something that most people in the room missed. They heard it, but Victor clued us in on one of his most valuable skills. Before I tell you what it is, let me tell you a fraction of his accomplishments. He held similar positions for The District of Columbia and for Arlington County (DC Adjacent), where he brought in billions of dollars, tens of thousands of jobs, a baseball stadium, malls, waterfront revitalization etc. He also brought Amazon to Arlington County, changing the economic face of an entire city. His job is to convince companies to invest in the area while competing with other jurisdictions, fighting just as hard for the same resources.

He wins. He wins consistently. He wins big.

"You know I talk a big game. I talked a lot tonight. But when I am trying to influence a global organization, a local government or anyone with my perspective, I listen first. I can sit in a meeting for an hour and not say a word. I learn their goals, their challenges, their reservations. I listen to the language they use. Then I incorporate everything I learned in my presentation. They hear my idea ... in their language. Listening is the key."

Boom.

I want you to learn from Victor. I want you to know your friends, your perceived enemies, your competitors as well as you know your product or service. Every person in the entire organization is your customer.

IT'S NOT PLAYING POLITICS. IT IS CREATING RELATIONSHIP.

> # ATTITUDE ADJUSTMENT
> Your job is to create allies and neutralize enemies.

The case for this is easy:

- Promotions and opportunity.
- Support when you need it (even when you don't know you need it).
- An awesome environment filled with people who you like, who like you and are fun to be around.
- A winning team.

Do you have that person you dread seeing or working with? It's just no fun.

Do you have a nemesis? Even less fun.

Let's Reflect

Making it real.

- Who are your allies?
- Who are your friendly competitors?
- Who is your nemesis?

Seth is VP of Operations. He has been working his way up for 6 years, loves the team, loves the work. In comes Andrea, a new CIO. Andrea is awesome and her addition lit up the team. She's also focused and demanding, and she stepped on Seth's toes more than once in her short time there. Seth has a little chip on his shoulder for working his way up and feeling like people still see him as "less than." It's made up in his head but feels very real. We talk about his trigger every few weeks and it is diminishing. Andrea sets it off easily with a quick comment or email. To be fair, she is a bit territorial as she establishes her own place in the organization. It's so tempting to look for ways Andrea is being "disrespectful." Since Seth has been there and has social credibility, he can easily turn people against her. He's slipped a few times.

Mark: "The CEO's plan and our goal is for you to be elevated to the Senior Leadership Team next year, right?"

Seth: "Yes."

Mark: "Andrea is on that team? She going anywhere soon?"

Seth: "Nope." He got it immediately. "F*ck! I know what you are going to say. I know she's great. I'm just being petty. Old habits are coming up. I'll shut up."

I'm silent.

Seth: "I know, I know, stop taking the bait when she's dismissive of me. Make her an ally. Help her in her new role." He jumped in with both feet.

Over a few months Andrea and Seth had to have numerous conversations. Seth had to set boundaries and make agreements on how they and their teams would work together. Seth had to have "the conversation" a few times:

The Conversation:

"When you did (observable behavior), the impact on my team was (specific and clear result), and in the future I'd like you to do (new explicit agreement)."

Write that down. Make "The Conversation" SOP.

Back to your list.

Time to work on the enemy list.

General rule for turning around a relationship with a difficult person:

- Create an empathy map.
- Take 100% responsibility (for your side of the street)

- ○ How did I create, or what behaviors contributed to this person (in this way) in my world?

  ○ What can they teach me?

  ○ Read Byron Katie's *Loving What Is*

- Check your ego (right or effective).

  ○ Deal with what's real not made up by your monkey mind

  ○ Don't waste time on lost causes or the unimportant

  ○ The world isn't fair, don't waste time on it, deal with what is

  ○ Don't try to win respect – be respectable

- Protect yourself (boundaries/agreements/feedback).

  ○ Be clear and direct in your communications

- Document Accomplishments

  ○ Document conversations

Have a look at the Nemesis Empathy Worskhseet when you are dealing with this section. (Link at the end of every chapter.)

By the way … there is nothing wrong with being the one person a difficult co-worker isn't difficult with.

It is so much easier to fall back on our very human behavior when working with strong personalities in a pressure filled environment.

It seems so many "get away" with bad behavior and succeed.

I am a big believer in karma, or the world reflecting back what you put out. With other people's behavior and circumstance, we see the tip of the iceberg. We don't know their actual experience of life. I get to see a lot of the iceberg and I can tell you; people reap what they sow.

Be the change you want to see in the world and watch your world change.

For access to worksheets and other resources go to
https://bit.ly/46r8u8u

Chapter 6

RELATIONSHIPS FIRST

---

*"Stay curious, stay vulnerable, stay kind,
adjust always, repair often, reset as needed."*

~ Michael Bungay Stanier

"LEADERSHIP WOULD BE EASY IF IT WEREN'T FOR PEOPLE."

The above is a lighthearted joke I share with my clients because almost every challenge we need to work through is … a people challenge.

I just got back from a family reunion with old folks, young folks, and some brand-new baby folks. There was a ton of love flowing. There was also a lot of family dynamics underlying the entire event. The longer it went on, the more overt those dynamics became.

It is inescapable.

If you haven't noticed, this entire book is about relationships. My goal is to help you level up your relationship skills, which will support your leadership skills.

THE BONUS: BETTER RELATIONSHIPS = BETTER LIFE.

I was in a deep work retreat for men a few years ago. These events are always filled with interesting characters. We start off strangers and by day two would die for each other because we've been sharing so intimately. It's a beautiful experience.

At this retreat, one guy was so abrasive and annoying even our best efforts to be kind and inclusive were tested. He came close to being asked to leave several times, but his earnestness and the goodwill of the group kept that from happening.

When it came time for him to share his story, the entire group of grown ass men were in tears. The story of childhood this man shared was filled with horrors none of us could imagine (and there were plenty of abused men in the group). Not only was his behavior forgotten at once, we were in awe that this man had a career, was raising a family, and living a productive life after what he'd endured. The love and bond that formed, the hugs this man got, the empathy and understanding in that space were more than he had ever experienced. To this day, it is still one of the most profound moments of my life.

A healthy team will out-perform a smart team and strong relationships are the way to do it.

Some general rules:

- Give the benefit of the doubt – assume good intention
- If not clear, ask.
- Lead with curiosity most of the time.
- Be clear in your communication and keep your word.

For access to worksheets and other resources go to
https://bit.ly/46r8u8u

Leading Your Team

SUCCESS THROUGH OTHERS

OWNERSHIP FOR YOUR
PEOPLE & CULTURE

MOVING FROM
OPERATIONAL TO
STRATEGIC

PRODUCTIVITY & RESULTS

LEADING YOUR TEAM

YOUR
LEADERSHIP
STYLE

MASTERING
YOUR
COMMUNICATION

ENGAGED & CONNECTED TEAM

Chapter 7

OPERATIONAL TO STRATEGIC

"Leadership is the single greatest factor in any team's performance. Whether a team succeeds or fails is all up to the leader.
The leader's attitude sets the tone for the entire team."

~ Jocko Willink

YOUR JOB IS LEADING NOT DOING

"My biggest mistake, in hindsight was, I felt like I was going to be the guy who made their jobs easier. I was going to help them be successful. I was taking on their problems and trying to clear their desks, so they could be "more productive." That's not the right move. What I ended up doing was exhausting myself, frustrating myself, not really enabling them to learn. I was stagnating their growth. I wanted to quit, you know, after two quarters, I had never worked so hard and been less successful. I honestly would lay awake at night, thinking about how I go to my boss to tell him, I want to go back to being a rep."

Kevin Haverty
The Rising Leader Podcast episode 13:
"Rising from Super Sales Rep to Effective Leader"
https://bit.ly/3MPXafp

Congratulations, you have the responsibility of being the CEO. Okay, not the actual CEO of the company, but you are the leader of your world, within the context of the broader organization. The buck stops with you.

I'm being intentionally a little flippant, because I know you understand this. But I need to tell you, you don't *really* understand it; not the full extent of how much responsibility you have taken on.

Every single leader I coach, each one I interview, and all those I've met are united by the fact that they underestimate how much people time leading involves.

Leading takes time. A lot of time. More time than you expect, *and* depending on your personality type, more than you think it should.

Three fundamental things change in direct proportion to how many people are on your team.

1. It's no longer your job to "do".

2. It's your job to motivate, inspire, train, grow, and focus your team.

3. It is your job to craft the vision, strategy and the culture of the folks who work in your department.

Whether you have The Dream Team or the Island of Misfit Toys, you will have to get the job done with the hand you are dealt. The hand you are dealt are your people, resources, and political capital.

We call this "Success Through Others." You can look at that as a drag on your productivity (go fast, go alone) or as a lever for greater success (go far, go together).

"I studied the Indigenous Australians and the Fijian Islanders and I asked the tribal leaders what their number one responsibility was. They said, "Our job is to teach the tribe to survive. If we were to go back in time, and observe a tribal meeting of Indigenous Australians, they would be teaching the younger tribe members to throw a boomerang. Why? Because if you weren't competent with throwing a boomerang, the chances of survival were low, the boomerang was the tool of survival.

So as leaders, our job is to teach people to throw the appropriate boomerang to be able to survive. It's not about who you bring in, but it's about how you nurture them."

Garry Ridge, former CEO WD-40
The Rising Leader Podcast episode 14:
"The Heart of a Servant-Leader"
https://bit.ly/3Gi89uf

Remember, leadership is not natural. Every promotion and increase in responsibilities will need new skills and mindsets. You will grow into it. Hopefully, you have received some training on the way to your current position. If not, you can learn on the job. Most do. Maybe leading a team, developing people, creating a culture of communication and accountability is already your strength. Awesome. Then you know it is still a constant evolution.

If you are like most fast-rising leaders, you got here because you outworked and out maneuvered everyone else. Navigating the people challenges may have felt like drag to YOUR success, even though it is part of your job.

Few will (seem to) work as hard as you.

Few will (seem to) be as sharp as you.

Few will (seem to) be as hyper-responsible as you.

It shouldn't be this way, but it is.

"Can't everyone just do their job without the drama?" If you hear yourself saying (or thinking) this" it may be a clue that you are arguing with the reality of your job as a leader.

At this level, that's got to change.

ATTITUDE ADJUSTMENT

Your peoples' problems are now your problem. Or said another way, "Your people are your job." Leadership is an actual job!

Earlier in your leadership career, you probably leaned on the "player coach," role. You were able to work alongside your folks, fixing problems late into the night, picking up the slack. The higher you go, the less "player" bandwidth you will have. You will not survive, let alone thrive if you don't learn to create exponential impact by leading your team. It is one of the harder lessons for me to drill into my younger clients.

"Mark, I can't deal with the drama and the problems people create," my client complains.

Let's say you are a teacher in a preschool. Hard to imagine, I know. It's not for me either. But all day every day, you are navigating tired kids. Hungry kids. Kids who need to get outside and blow off steam. Kids who won't share. Kids with abusive parents. Kids with over- indulgent parents. Kids with special needs. Man, we need to pay teachers more, right? Anyway, your job is to teach them, keep them safe and create some sort of order and fun out of the chaos. Do you admonish the kids? Blame them for being tired or hungry or needing time on the jungle gym? No, you take a deep breath and stay big. You keep perspective. You take a breather to collect yourself when it gets too much. You lean on the other teachers. Because the kids don't know any better and it's your job to teach them. Same with your team. I don't mean to reduce them to cranky children, but for this exercise I need to be stark. You don't have the luxury of joining the fray or complaining about reality. With adults you have more tools. You can reason (mostly), coach and expect more of a partnership in building the order and fun of this business classroom. But people are going to people. Accept it. You can change the ones out who refuse to grow. But usually, not immediately. You have to play the hand you are dealt. Your job is to create a great hand. Remember Jocko – no bad teams, just bad leaders."

Your job is leadership now. You are becoming a student in the school of creating better people who in turn create greater impact. Moving from an operational mindset to a strategic focus comes with a few potholes. Every new way of being takes time to adjust. As your team starts to hum along, you may feel useless.

You may also experience:

- Knowing less than some of your folks about the specifics.
- Feeling like things are a bit out of your control.
- Finding yourself having difficult conversations, daily.
- Asking questions and find yourself listening, a lot.
- Knowing way more about your people's personal lives than you think necessary or comfortable.

It's time to think of yourself as "coach" versus "boss".

I remember when I threw my hat in the ring to be sales manager in one of the start-ups I worked for. The Area Director offered an Attitude Adjustment: "To be a successful sales leader you need to want to see other people succeed more than yourself. If not, it will be a struggle every day."

Wise words.

The best leaders know they work for their people (without doing their work). They KNOW their accolades come from their folks shining, not from the spotlight being on them. You may know it on paper, but in practice it is counterintuitive to your ego. You may need time to make this adjustment. Most people do.

Once accepted, it is one of the most rewarding experiences in life.

Every great leader, when asked to reflect on their career, shares story after story of their impact on people.

"The team took me through everything. The team put me on their shoulders. You know, the team made it work. They literally cared about our level of excellence. They cared about how things made me look. It was one of the greatest experiences of my life.

And I think it was an ability to work with the team, to care about the team, to inspire a team, and to be inspired by a team, that creates those at bats. I didn't have to stand at the plate wondering if just being the world's greatest athlete was gonna get me through the day, that wasn't it. I stood at the plate, knowing that I had an entire team that was going to make sure that we swung at the right things and that we got the right at bats.

And it was an incredibly humbling experience to know that my career was in the hands of a lot of people. And to be very comfortable with that, and not worry about going into a room and routinely understand that I was not the smartest person in the room."

Larry Quinlan
The Rising Leader Podcast episode 34:
"Leadership, Humility and Success"
https://bit.ly/3sICyie

"I'm talking about science. Emerging science that says that our hearts are not just the pump. That there's a connection between the heart and the mind, that the heart sends more communication to the mind than the other way around. What we feel and experience is experienced through our bodies and our hearts, informing our minds on the choices we make.

So, if you want to be engaged, if you want people to be engaged at work, if you want people to be highly productive and loyal, you're going to have to do the things that affect the heart in a positive way. That will influence them naturally. It's so compelling when you hear it that way. When I talk about this, people go "G-d, no, you don't do that because they'll take advantage of you, they won't do their work, you'll never meet their goals.""

I say, "Who told you that? Hasn't been my experience."

Mark C. Crowley
The Rising Leadership Podcast episode 22:
"Leading from the Heart"
https://bit.ly/3Rgl1ar

Let's get to know your team:

I remember reading in a parenting book that "the instructions for raising your kid are written on their ass." Each kid is different and needs different parenting.

I have one son who will not spend money. Baseball was his life, and it was a fight to let me buy him a new glove when he outgrew his old one. One day, I found $4,000 in his nightstand draw. I asked if he was dealing drugs or something. "You know I haven't spent a dime since I was 5 years old." My other son was at Chipotle with his friends every day. Like his dad, shiny and new was the order of the day. There was lint, a paper clip, and no money in his drawer. Two sons, two different teachings about money.

Your folks are no different. The instructions for leading and coaching your team members are written on their forehead. That means you may have to be a different kind of leader for each person. Think of your job as a leader as a character in a play, it will help you expand the range of how you show up.

Remember, your personality type or leadership style is a box of how you've been. You are not a static, fixed mindset kind of person. You are dynamic, growing, and flexible.

"Leadership is learned." You will get better and better.

- List the names of all your team members.
- Write down who needs what to be successful.
- It could be:

- ○ Resources
- ○ Training
- ○ Coaching
- ○ Reassurance
- ○ Time off to care for family
- ○ Difficult feedback
- ○ Recognition
- ○ Something else?

It's your job to find out what your people need to be successful, and get it for them.

Dan Warmenhoven (CEO) and Tom Mendoza (President) set a unique culture at NetApp, one of the first start-ups I worked for. They set out a goal but did not dictate how the goal should be accomplished. Instead, they asked, "What do you need to be successful." And got it for them.

SETTING THE VISION FOR **YOUR** DEPARTMENT

Time to get out your notebook:

- What is the mission of the company?
- How does YOUR team fit into the larger organization?
- How do you see YOUR team fulfilling/contributing to the overall mission?
- What does success look like?
- What does your team actually do today?
- How will you achieve your goals?
- What is the gap?
- Who do we want to be? (What kind of people/team rock this vision?)

- How do we want to be seen? (How do we want the larger organization to talk about us?)

- How do we want to go about our business? (Aspirational attitude)

CREATING YOUR CULTURE OR TEAM SPIRIT

"If you're really asking people to give you their heart and soul, and go all in, makes sure they know you appreciate and respect them. I came out with the saying "catch someone doing something right" at the end of 94, We started to grow real fast and I couldn't keep track so I said, "if you see someone do something extraordinary to help NetApp, to help a customer, help a partner, to help society, let me know and I call them directly." About 80% was peer to peer. I viewed that as viral culture building. I made sure, if someone said something, I would always call.

Bill McDermott is a great leader at ServiceNow. He was SAP CEO. He asked me how I found the time to make the calls? I averaged 10 calls a day over a 15-year period. They last probably 30 seconds for a message or five minutes for a call.

I would say, "I want to let you know, we're proud of you." Then I may ask them how they are doing. It may go on for two minutes. When you're not expecting a call from the President of the company, it actually feels like a long call. And you know what, I got as much more out of it than the other person because I learned about them or a customer or the company."

Tom Mendoza, Former President/Vice Chair NetApp
The Rising Leader Podcast episode 30:
"People-Centered Leadership"
https://bit.ly/3GBX3Rb

Remember, much of this may cascade from the leadership team or CEO. If the overall company has done a good job of this, *your job is easier.* Either way, YOU need to be clear for your TEAM to be clear.

"I have an algorithm:

Culture = Values + Behavior X Consistency.

As a leader, you have to have a clearly defined set of values that people understand. Those values are there to not only protect people but set them free. We say in the organization, you can make just about any decision on your own, as long as you use our values as your filter.

The next one is behavior. Leaders have to love their people enough and as a leader be brave enough. What do I mean by that? They have to love them enough to recognize them for doing great work. They have to love them enough to praise them when they need to, but they have to be brave enough to also redirect them as needed. They need to do that in the caring way. Empathy has got to come into play.

A lot of people think that culture in an organization is about taking some fairy dust and sprinkling it over their organization. It's not; it's not that at all. You need to consistently walk with them."

Garry Ridge
The Rising Leader Podcast episode 14:
"The Heart of a Servant-Leader"
https://bit.ly/3Gi89uf

HOW'S YOUR DELEGATION GAME?

You know you should. You know the benefits.

- Frees you up to do the things you are supposed to be doing as a leader.
- Math - exponential impact
- There are people on your team who are better than you at certain tasks.
- Create new leaders in the organization by giving your team the opportunity to step up.

But why don't you?

Let's Reflect

Write down everything on your list that *should* be delegated.

What are the seemingly legitimate reasons you don't delegate as much as you should?

- My team is over-worked enough already.
- They won't do it as well as I can.
- I will have to redo everything.
- What will I do?

You can refer to your "personality assessment" for attributes that have you hesitate delegating.

Control, standards, and excessive empathy could all be habitual mindsets that will sabotage your team's productivity and effectiveness.

Let's go back to the list and qualify each item that you put in the *should be delegated* column:

- Pick one item that has been hard to let go.
- Who is the best person or team to handle it?
- What is your objection and what can you do to address your concerns?
  - Training?
  - Check ins?
  - Let it go?

- What does "done" look like?
- Decide to delegate it.
- Communicate clearly with agreements from the list above.

You will need to train yourself to be patient with iteration and coaching. The delegation – feedback loop is an ongoing skill to master. Over time you will be empowering your team, helping them level up, and creating exponential leverage to create results.

DELEGATE TO DEVELOP

"Lesson number two is leaders get no bullets. I get a lot of pushback on this until people really understand it. We train young leaders, who have made it onto Seal Teams, to lead in a gunfight. Their job is to maneuver the team around the target and take out the target.

It usually goes like this: We're walking through the woods, or desert and these targets pop up and start shooting at us. We start engaging the target and those young leaders, 100% of the time, also start engaging the target bam, bam bam bam, bam, bam, bam, bam, bam, and start knocking things down and they're doing a great job.

Except they're not leading.

Their job is not to look down the sights of their weapon and engage the target, their job is to look at the enemy, look at the friendly forces, look at the terrain and make a decision.

So after two or three runs, I'll position myself next to that brand new leader and let them fail, let them do the thing that they're doing. Now is my opportunity to shoot and engage the targets and do the fun stuff. But then I yell to them, "hey, what's a call? Hey, what's a call? Hey, what's a call?" And they're still shooting. And they yell back "I don't know," and keep shooting.

So eventually I take their bullets away. I say "you get to go out there but you get no bullets. And they feel absolutely neutered. I've taken their manhood away and they hate me. And that's okay. Because now when the contact happens, when we start getting in the gunfight, they can't shoot because they don't have any bullets. Now they have to do their job. So now they're paying attention to the enemy situation, the friendly situation, the terrain.

If they get a kind of get stuck, I might help them and ask, "what about that hillside over there. And I'm still shooting 'cause I know the call. I know what needs to happen because I've done it 1000 times. Eventually, they start making the right calls. And then eventually, I'll give them their bullets back. But in the beginning, they get no bullets.

If you're looking down the sights of your weapon, and you're engaging the target, there's zero perspective, there's zero chance to actually lead. You need to step back, detach yourself from the gunfight. Look around. Figure out what to do now."

William Branum,
veteran Navy SEAL, founder Naked Warrior Recovery
The Rising Leader Podcast episode 18:
"The Navy SEAL Secrets to Leadership"
https://bit.ly/3vmuPY6

Your job is to create additional leaders. Delegation is a great tool to train, coach, and prepare your team members for that next step.

Let's look at your team. You may already have evaluations you can rely on. The important thing is to take time to reflect and plan.

- List down the names of each of your team members.

- For each person list their top 2 or 3 strengths and weaknesses.

- Are they in the right role?

- Does their current role leverage their strengths in the best way possible?

- What additional responsibilities can they take on to develop their career and impact though their strengths.

We need to remember that strengths and weaknesses are contextual. They are not judgments of worth or value.

- Delegate to leverage strengths: delegate things you know they can do well and with high standards.

- Delegate to develop weaknesses: delegate things you know they need to learn with modified expectations and be available to handhold them through the process and offer coaching and feedback.

If you are nervous about a particular project, try this progression:

"Let's do it together."

"Go do this, and let's review each step."

"This is yours; I trust you."

Delegation is an art AND a science. You will not get it right all of the time. You will delegate things that should have had more oversight and that is okay. Expect mistakes and work through them.

Watch your impact improve and your people shine.

As with feedback and difficult conversations, be wary of being too harsh or too affable. This story from our Kim Scott interview brought it home for me beautifully.

"Someone sent me an article that said, "People would rather have a boss who's a total asshole, but really competent than one who's really nice, but incompetent. And I thought, why are they sending me this, they think I'm a jerk, or they think I'm incompetent? Surely, those are not my two choices. That was the moment when I really started wrestling with this because there must be a third way right? There must be a way where you can both care and challenge at the same time.

Around that same time I had gotten a puppy. I loved this puppy and I loved her so much, I had never said a cross word to her. As a result, she was totally out of control. I'm taking her for a walk one night and she jumps in front of a speeding cab. I pulled her out of the way in the nick of time, and a man was watching. He said, "I can tell you really love that dog, but, you're gonna kill that dog if you don't teach her to sit." And then he said, "Sit!" The dog sat. I had no idea she even knew what that meant. I kind of looked up at him in amazement. He said, "It's not mean; it's clear." And then the light change, he walked off, leaving me with a way out of my conundrum. I could continue to be kind, but also give people very direct feedback."

Kim Scott
Mastering Overwhelm Podcast episode 22:
"The Art of Radical Candor"
https://bit.ly/3RgOO2T

For access to worksheets and other resources go to
https://bit.ly/46r8u8u

Chapter 8

YOUR LEADERSHIP STYLE

HOW WELL DOES YOUR TEAM REALLY KNOW YOU?

"I called the book, *Lead from the Heart,* because in our world, there's no heart. There's simply no heart in business. It's all about the mind, rational thinking, and analytics. We're not thinking about the human, right? I believe we have to bring the heart and the mind into balance.

I'm not saying take the mind out of this. I'm not saying don't do the data, I'm not saying don't hold people accountable for their performance, weed them out, if they're not performing. I'm just saying you don't have to be ruthless about it. When we use the phrase "the real world," question what the real world is. That's what I did. I found out that in the real world,

people really want a boss that they can trust, that cares about them, and who wants the best for them. Someone who is an ambassador and coach for them. They may not express it to you, but it's true.

Mark C. Crowley
The Rising Leadership Podcast episode 22:
"Leading from the Heart "
https://bit.ly/3Rgl1ar

In Leading Up you filled out a Boss Empathy Map so you could understand who and what you are dealing with. In Leading Across I suggested the same thing for the leadership team members because understanding the playing field is your greatest advantage.

Understanding yourself is your second greatest advantage. We do this with self-reflection, personality assessments, and interviews etc. Once you understand yourself, you can teach your team how best to *work with you.*

When your team understands you and how you work you have created another powerful advantage. If they understand how best to communicate with you, they will feel more confident, be more open and effective. You will have a more pleasant day as the friction of miscommunication lessons.

This is a great time to pull out any of the assessments and feedback you have gotten over the last couple of years.

What story do they tell of you as a leader?

- What strengths do you bring to the table?
- How well do you leverage those strengths?
- What are your challenges?
- What are your blind spots?

Use the exercises and examples of other leaders from Leading Up to create a Boss Empathy Map on yourself. Which boss type or types resonate with your self description? Do you see gaps in your leadership? What books (many recommended here) or courses would help?

If you do not have this information already, this next exercise is a great start. We will also be going deeper into Knowing Yourself in the next section of this book.

Warning: this next exercise is not for the faint of heart. It is for those leaders who truly want to shine, excel, grow etc.

1. Have your team collectively fill out a Boss Empathy Map on you. (Great team building activity). Have them pick a leader and come up with only useful and constructive feedback. This is an earnest request for feedback, not a bitch session.

2. Additional useful questions

○ What would you like me to start doing that would be helpful?

○ What would you like me to stop doing?

○ What would you like me to continue doing that is working well?

3. Have them pick a primary boss style for you.

4. Do the same for yourself.

If you do not have previous reports and do not want to go through this exercise another way to get the info you need is by conducting an anonymous 360-like assessment.

An inexpensive and effective version I have use is www.spidergap.com.

After you deal with the shock of the feedback, (no ego likes feedback).

Let's Reflect

• How well does your team really know you?

• Were you surprised? How?

• What did you learn?

• Is your self-view different from your team's view?

• What boss style did they pick for you? For yourself?

• Why do you think they chose the style they did?

• What did you hate most about the feedback?

• What weakness or blind spot did this exercise uncover?

○ Was it a surprise?

• What strengths do you bring to the table as a leader?

○ Any pleasant surprises?

- Are you actually wrong about yourself or is it a function of communication?

William is the CEO of a $50M company of 70 employees. He built it from the ground up and like most entrepreneurs, he has a head for business, drive for success, and cares about his people. "Part of our mission is to create a great experience for our people," William says, and he means that. He loves the people who work for him and he feels responsible for their well-being. as well as that of their families.

He's as affable as they come. Everyone loves him. And, he is usually the smartest and most creative person in any conversation. He can fix anything given a whiteboard and some time.

They missed their target two quarters in a row and next quarter looks anemic. He was increasingly anxious about the troublesome trend.

He was sharing his communication in the last leadership team meeting with me and was about to move on in the conversation.

My stomach was tight … I almost let it go but then I said, "Did you use that tone of voice in the meeting?"

"I don't know, maybe."

Out on a limb now, "This is just my experience, so take it as that. From what I heard, you came across angry, mean, and very condescending. That's not who you are but I'm curious if that was the case."

"I was trying to explain to them the real challenge we were facing. I really wasn't mad at them. They couldn't work harder. I was mad at myself and frustrated with the situation."

"Hhhmmm. I have heard that tone before. With your sons. With your wife. And with me a few times. I'm not sure you know how intense of a presence you are." We have talked about some of his team being intimidated by how smart and driven he is. "When you are frustrated with yourself or a situation, it can feel like you are angry with us. And it comes out dripping with condescension." I hated saying that, but it was true.

This was a shock to his system. We had him go back and ask the folks he trusts and sure enough, that was reflected back to him.

In the next meeting he made amends. He also had conversations with his sons and wife, healing hurt he didn't even know he caused.

Now, when he feels that intensity, he just preferences his demeanor with, "If I sound harsh, I am not mad at you, just frustrated with the situation." That's all it takes. Of course, he is working on how he comes across, but while that shift is happening, he keeps everyone safe and clear.

We need that reflection from the world because our intention might not equal our impact.

WHAT TO DO WITH THE FEEDBACK

Armed with the research you already have or the new information from the above exercise, it's time to get some help.

This is a great opportunity to check in with your coach, significant other, friend or mentor. Go over the results and your thoughts with someone you trust. *You need an objective perspective.*

Tease out what's real, perceived, important and not so important. Ask yourself, "is this how I want to be seen?"

If not, let's start making some changes.

- Pick one thing you could start doing, or improving that would make the biggest impact.

- Pick the one thing you could stop doing or change the way you do it, that would make the biggest impact.

Communicate to your team and your boss that you will be working on these two areas. Thank them for their honesty and support (again) and prove you are a vulnerable, transparent, and powerful leader by taking the feedback like a champ, and doing something about it.

Remember, this is a powerful tool to create a culture of constructive feedback.

> ## YOUR JOB IS TO GET BETTER AS A LEADER.
> ## TO EXPAND YOUR RANGE.

ATTITUDE ADJUSTMENT

Your job is to be the leader your team need you to be in any given situation. If you find yourself digging in "I'm just this way," your opportunity for growth will be stunted.

Let's Reflect

- Take out that list of team members you made in the last chapter.
- Reflect on each in the context of how you lead.
- What do you see they might need from you that you didn't see before this conversation?
- What step can you take to accommodate their needs?

For access to worksheets and other resources go to
https://bit.ly/46r8u8u

Leading You

BEING YOUR BEST IN ALL SITUATIONS

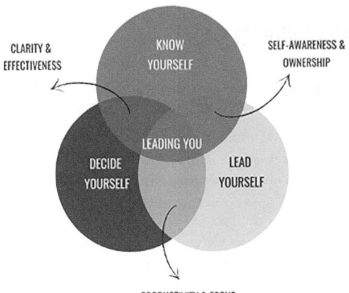

Chapter 9

KNOW YOURSELF

WHY KNOW YOURSELF? WHY DO THIS WORK AT ALL?

"One who conquers himself or herself is greater than another
who conquers a thousand men on the battlefield."
~ The Buddha

"He/she who rules his/her spirit has won a greater victory
than the taking of a city."
~Jesus

"One can have no smaller or greater mastery
than the mastery over one's self."
~Leonardo da Vinci

If you go to my website you will see a very polished video of my story. I'll save you some time: crippling self-hatred, addiction and undiagnosed A.D.D. lead to me becoming homeless, 135 pounds and living in my little red pick-up truck at the age of 27. I am forever grateful to my brother Barry for insisting I live with him, go to AA/NA, the gym, and take college classes. If not for him, I would not have gotten married, had two amazing sons, a college education, and a successful career.

I would not be writing this book.

Just yesterday I was speaking to a friend who is prone to depressive episodes. These episodes used to debilitate her for long stretches. She is now able to experience the triggers, thoughts and emotions and continue to function at a high level. She was in the middle of one and I was so inspired.

"You are bad ass! We are both bad asses. I know I shouldn't be here. I should be Nicholas Cage in *Leaving Las Vegas* spending my money on hookers, booze, and drugs. That's where my default takes me. You and I choose our tools every day. We choose our support. We choose to serve no matter how we feel. We know ourselves. We know our triggers, our tendencies, our strengths. We have spent a lifetime learning what routines and practices we need. We have built relationships that support us. We rock this life, faults and all."

That's what I want for you. I don't want you to just get by. I want you to thrive no matter your past or current challenges.

We are going to take the bundle of humanity that is you and turn it into a powerful leader who makes a positive impact on customers, employees, family members and everyone you meet.

By now, you have a good sense of who you are in each situation, as well as a roadmap of where to focus (on yourself) to have the biggest impact.

Yet, in order to really thrive, we need to go deeper.

How well do you actually know yourself? Most people know their Myers Briggs letters (I am an INFP) and will state them proudly when asked. From the time you were given a name, you were labeled, evaluated, judged, and molded by your parents, teachers, friends, circumstances, and society until the unique stew that is associated with your name was locked and loaded.

"We have our hard-wired survival biology, which is the fight or flight syndrome. If we don't survive life, then aspirations or creating doesn't matter. Every moment of our lives, the first dibs response, at every moment, is our fear-based survival instinct. It's hardwired into us for self, physical, and emotional preservation because that's paramount. That's the highest priority because the difference between life or death can be a split second, which is faster than we can think.

It's there because we need something that can work on our behalf to save us in these moments of critical exposure. It does that very well. Examples might be, well, if you drive a car through an intersection, somebody runs a red light, and if it t-boned you everybody gets killed, yet somehow you turn away from it. You could not think fast enough to do that. But something's listening, that enable that to happen that was faster than you can think. That physical, biological survival mechanism shows up when you feel under siege or under threat by someone that said something that was very provocative or very aggressive. Then you found yourself saying something back so quick that you don't remember even thinking about what you were going to say? But you said it.

Then there is what I call the Champion's Mind, the living, breathing mind organism that thinks, interprets, routes, stores, edits, conveys information in a very thoughtful and deliberate way, when we're given an opportunity. This is optimistic, there's plenty of room for everybody, where we can all win and celebrate each other's wins.

So, you can see that there are these contrasting ideas that are always there.

The point I'd like to make here is that you can't shut this (survival self) off, because if this is part of our biology, then it's going to be on our entire life.

It's a battle that we have to recognize and understand because if we identify with the survival self as the real us, rather than the Champion's Mind, then we are destined to a life of mediocrity."

Dr. Jeff Spencer
The Rising Leader Podcast episode 37:
"Playing the Bigger Game"
https://bit.ly/3QVeCQL

There is a "conditioned self" and a "transcendent self," as Dr. Spencer explains above. The practices in the previous sections of this book were to designed to get you to identify your habitual reactions, and to pause then create a new and different response.

This is what Jeff Spencer is talking about and what we will explore in this section.

When I start a coaching relationship I say: "Tell me your story."

I want to know how this human was formed so when behaviors and reactions present themselves, we have a roadmap of beliefs and conditioning that contribute to how the story played itself out.

So much of how we perceive the world and the way we respond to it can be directly linked to ages 0 through 7.

Historians are mixed on whether it was Aristotle or the Jesuits who said, *Give me a child until he is seven years old, and I will show you the man.* Behavioral phycologists show data that our subconscious makes up about 90-95% of who we present ourselves to be in the world, and maybe 5% is consciously, deliberately us.

We are basically lab rats running a maze or hitting a bell for cheese. Sorry, I don't make the rules, I've just been studying and living it for decades. The more I learn, the more I see it is true.

"We are not in relationship with the world, we are in relationship with what we *think* about the world." It's the "think" part that untrustworthy.

Depressing huh?

At first, yes. It is like the FedEx Logo. Once you see the arrow between the E and the X, you can no longer un-see it.

I was sitting on my meditation cushion one morning, and all the sudden I saw it. I saw what every spiritual teacher had been trying to tell me.

One moment I was "Mark," struggling to quiet my mind, then the next it all fell away. I saw that my personality, who I thought I was, was a product of experience and choices and what I made from them. Mark was made up. Made up of a lifetime of experiences, reactions, decisions, beliefs, traumas, joys. Mark never existed. Mark was/is a made-up concept. What was real was the moment. Life. What is. Mark was the interface.

For days after this I reeled. My kids. My clients. My spouse. All life in a person-colored wrapper.

I was so shaken I called Teo Alfero who is a shamanic practitioner and spiritual teacher that I mentioned earlier in the book. "Teo, Mark doesn't exist. I am about to teach a time management workshop and time doesn't exist. What do I do? Why do any of this?"

Teo said, "Welcome to the club," in his cool AF Argentinian accent, "Now we play."

And there was the freedom. The heaviness lifted. Mark, time, clients, book writing, workshops, relationships all exist as playdough. Every interaction, everything we can be play.

What I want to drive home from that little side trip into the land of Woo is this:

Don't take this all so seriously. Your job, your circumstances, your personality, your stories. Most of your stress comes from pressure you make up between your ears.

This isn't a book on the nature of human consciousness ... it is a handbook for you to be your best in all situations. I did want to wet your appetite for the freedom deeper contemplation offers though.

If you want to dive deeper on this topic, I have compiled a list of some of my favorite books on my website. I have separated the selections into separate sections, Spiritual, Leadership and Self Help/Coaching:

HTTPS://WWW.MARKJSILVERMAN.COM/SUGGESTED-BOOKS

I have had several, balls-to-the-wall, Type-A clients dip their toe into this topic to find true freedom from the monkey mind and the rat race. I would be remiss to not offer you the same off ramp.

This is a good time to take a walk, contemplate what I just shared and file it for later. Exploring consciousness and humanity is a life-long journey. For our purposes, I just want you to see that whoever you think you are, you are fungible. As we explore "how you show up," and the traits you tend to exhibit, remember that you can influence them. You can change and grow, transform even, now that I have shown you that you are NOT your box.

Let's look at the box you've been living and working in much of the time.

THE BOX: PERSONALITY TESTS AND ASSESSMENTS

You may have taken any number of "personality" tests similar to Myers Briggs to learn your work style, unique talents and where you fit on a team. I have a love/hate relationship with the idea that an assessment can put you in a box with specific attributes. I have seen people get pretty protective about their box. For me, the purpose of defining the box is to see tendencies, uncover the conditioning, as I mentioned above. Once conscious, we can work to expand our range far beyond the box.

I tend to not be a detail person. I know that about myself. Yet when a situation calls for detailed attention, I can take a deep breath and dive in. I can also hire someone to take care of the details, distill the details, and minimize how much that is part of my day.

I stopped saying, "I don't" or "I can't do details." (I just hate them ☺).

Look at your box. Understand your box. Know you are not your box, and these tools will be invaluable.

Enneagram: The fundamental premise of the Enneagram is that each of us has one dominant (not exclusive) energy that drives us in everything we do. This dominant energy is our greatest gift, so if we use it too much it can become our chief fault. This energy, like a prevailing wind that bends a tree permanently, sculpts our inner terrain and shapes our entire life. The Enneagram map depicts what model of the universe each of nine different kinds of people live in.

https://www.integrative9.com

1– Strict Perfectionist

2– Considerate Helper

3– Competitive Achiever

4– Intense Creative

5– Quiet Specialist

6– Loyal Sceptic

7– Enthusiastic Visionary

8– Active Controller

9– Adaptive Peacemaker

I have all my clients learn their Enneagram type and meet with an Enneagram master coach because I have found it to be profoundly accurate and useful. I myself am a certified Enneagram coach.

DiSC: DiSC is an acronym that stands for the four main personality profiles described in the DiSC model: (D)ominance, (i)nfluence, (S)teadiness, and (C)onscientiousness. People with D personalities tend to be confident and place an emphasis on accomplishing bottom-line results.

DiSC is one of the most prominent models used in business settings.

https://www.123test.com/disc-personality-test/

Strength Finder 2.0: This tool supports the premise that we should forget about fixing our weaknesses, and go all in on our strengths instead, by showing you ways to figure out which 5 key strengths are an innate part of you and giving you advice on how to use them in your life and work.

https://www.amazon.com/StrengthsFinder-2-0-Tom-Rath

Wealth Dynamics: Many people think that there are hundreds of routes to wealth. With Wealth Dynamics, you'll see that there are actually only eight paths to wealth and that one of those paths is the correct one for you.

The Creator, Mechanic, Star, Supporter, Deal Maker, Trader, Accumulator

https://www.wealthdynamics.com

Though Wealth Dynamics' language focuses on wealth creation, it is an amazing tool for finding your strengths and more natural abilities, and to learn what you need in a partner and additional team members.

Working Genius Model: Leadership author Patrick Lencioni, author of *The Five Dysfunctions of a Team*, created *Working Genius* to help individuals and teams discover their gifts and transform their work.

https://bit.ly/3Sj71gV

Working Genius is one of the newer entries into the assessments mix. I have experimented with a few leadership teams using this model and the feedback has been very positive. I plan to make this a regular part of my practice.

Your Five Love Languages: This one has broad applicability for work, friends, family, or romance. Some of us like to be praised, some rewarded, and some of us need a hug. Good to know about yourself and an easy gift to give to those around you.

https://5lovelanguages.com

HOW DOES YOUR "BOX" SHOW UP IN THE REAL WORLD?

While we spend time being introspective, we also need to learn the client's impact in the "real world." The most effective tool I use for this in my coaching is the 360-degree feedback review which is a process through which feedback from an employee's subordinates, peers, colleagues, and supervisor(s), as well as a self-evaluation by the employee themselves is gathered. Such feedback can also include, when relevant, feedback from external sources who interact with the employee, such as customers and suppliers or other interested stakeholders. The 360-degree feedback is so named because it solicits feedback regarding an employee's behavior from a variety of points of view. I offered a sample in "Your Leadership Style" called Spidergap.

Criticism isn't easy. Even if the feedback is 98% glowing and 2% growth areas, human nature is to focus on the negative.

One client, Beth, had a hard time with the feedback.

"Give me three words describing Beth on a bad day."

"Grumpy, short, stressed, closed, impatient, angry, attacking, condescending ..."

"How many bad days does Beth have a week?"

"Three or four."

"Oh!"

This was the consensus of six interviews.

Beth was actually immune to the criticisms of her behavior initially. She wore her aggressive style as a badge of honor (her childhood story would make it understandable). She is brilliant, effective, and invaluable so she didn't need to change in her past roles. That changed when she became a C-Suite executive with the impact and responsibility that entails.

She knew she had bad days ... but when she heard "3 or 4 days a week" she became silent. As she reflected over the next week, she realized how tightly wound she was. She realized that although her style kept her safe (in her mind) that it also kept her lonely. She realized that most of her week was spent unhappy.

Beth began to notice the water she was swimming in and realized she didn't like it. Not only did it make the team miserable (consciousness is a bitch), she *was* miserable. And she didn't want to be miserable anymore.

We started working on external behaviors and saw immediate improvement. There were still flashes of anger and even when she had it "under control," people could feel it. She learned to fix situations she relapsed in and to self-deprecate when the tension was obvious.

While better, it still wasn't the level of emotional maturity the role needed, and she was increasingly aware of how it affected her and her family.

Conditioning is tough to break, as we discussed earlier. If you truly want to change, you must do the deep work. Therapy, experiential weekends and retreats, meditation, journaling, trauma work all help to get at the root cause of emotions and behaviors.

Beth is on her way to healing. With the tools she has learned from therapy she is able to communicate better. I still get calls to talk her off the ledge, which is great. A 5-minute call with your coach can set your wheels back under you quickly.

Personally, I have found that the deeper I dig to root out the unconscious that is running my life, the freer I am. I want that for you as well.

I have found few tools as useful as a well-researched and communicated 360 review.

HANDLE YOURSELF! TRIGGERS.

Take a minute and reflect on what pisses you off. What people, places, situations trigger you.

Trigger: A response to people, places, or situations that send you into an overly emotional response. It will often show up as "fight or flight," the need to run, freeze or fight.

It can look like anger, shut down, numbing, or bypassing.

The challenge is that it is automatic and you feel you have no control over your reaction.

Remember, if someone reacts more than a 4 on the scale from 1-10, it is usually something other than the presenting thing. Triggers are the same. Once triggered, there is little you can do, the body takes over and the damage is done.

And, you can learn to anticipate situations and be ready with a tool. You can recover more quickly and minimize the damage. You can also do the deep work at another time to figure out what the heck is actually happening.

Let's Reflect

Paper and pen time.

Write down a list of the people and situations that have triggered you in the past. These are the things that are a 5 and above.

Your job now is to slow them down to see what you made them mean to have an outsized reaction.

When I do live workshops I often tell a dog story that goes like this ...

You're walking down the street, and let's say you're Data from Star Trek, and you have no thoughts, feelings or emotions. You see a dog. A dog is a dog. Seeing it provokes nothing in you; it has no associations. But let's say that growing up you helped raise puppies or foster rescues. When you see a dog your heart is in your throat. You love dogs. You say, "can I pet your dog, please?"

If you have a reason to be afraid of dogs you won't see a fluffy four-legged friend, you'll see a fierce oversized animal with its teeth bared. The perception problem is that we don't see dogs, we run everything through a filter of our beliefs, experiences and conditionings. Everything that has happened to us impacts our perception.

We scare ourselves every day, all day. Things like the emails in our inbox can push us into fight or flight. In pre-modern times when confronted with a saber- toothed tiger the appropriate response was to freeze, run or hide. There was something you could do about the situation. In our time, we're not often in physical danger yet the physiological responses still trigger because we turn things into saber-toothed tigers. For me, it's my taxes. As soon as my my accountant calls me and says, "Hey Mark, can you go into the portal and check this document?" Suddenly I don't even know where the portal is and I go into flight. I've turned my taxes a prehistoric tiger. You do that all day long.

Remember, everything gets put through your filter of beliefs, experiences, and conditioning. Everything.

What did you turn into a saber tooth tiger? Nine times out of 10, your response is from fear. Remember, anger is a secondary emotion. Sadness or fear are almost always under anger.

Shut down is fear. Rage is fear. Numbing is fear (of feeling).

- All fear comes from an imagined future.
- BUT your body reacts as if the danger is real.
- You are in fight or flight, where the only options are fight, run, or hide.
- There is no creativity. No options. No vision.

Let's take one of the items you put on your triggered list and examine it.

What happened (that a video camera would see)? She raised her voice at me. He pointed out my mistake in front of the entire team.

What did you make it mean? He disrespected me. They called me out for screwing up. They kept me in the dark.

How are you scaring yourself? This is often internal self-talk. I looked weak/incompetent. They are cutting me out. They know I'm a fraud. I'm sure you have a playlist of greatest hits.

Is it true? I mean, beyond a shadow of a doubt, true?

What's real now? What can you know for sure. Usually, it is what is captured on the imaginary video. Here is where you list what is truer than your interpretation. She's under pressure, it wasn't about me. I was left off the email by mistake. I am good at my job, and it was an honest mistake. Get curious.

Take a deep breath. This is some of the most profound work a person can do. If you can separate what you "think" about a situation and get closer to reality, you are on your way to intellectual and emotional maturity.

Where do you want to place your attention? This is where you engage your will. It takes effort to move your attention from your habitual thoughts to something new. They are cunning and seductive. Do you want to stay in the problem or create something new. It's crazy how often that question comes up when navigating new leadership challenges.

Actively choose.

What do you want to create now? I want to repair or get clarity on the situation. I want to focus on the next challenge. I want to set a boundary or create an agreement so there is no misunderstanding in the future.

Extra credit: If you are feeling brave, let's go a little deeper and ask one final question.

What do I have to believe in order to have reacted or felt that way?

Nothing can disturb you unless it lands on something you believe. If I call you a purple couch, you would roll your eyes and walk away. You KNOW you aren't a purple couch. But if I said you don't have a good handle on your team's work product ...

In order for it to get a reaction, you would have to believe that you are not up to the job. Or that people are devious and trying to oust you. It has to already be there to bother you.

I worked with one CEO who "shut down" in meetings with his own team when things got tense. It was weird. It was his company that he build from the ground up. He hand-picked the team and they worked together for years. But it was still a pattern.

We did some inquiry and he had an insight. When he was a kid, he was viciously ostracized from the gang of kids in his neighborhood. He never knew why, they just stopped playing with him and made fun of him when he walked by.

The filter that got created: "People will turn on you, even your friends."

And he brought that into the boardroom. He knew how to cover it up, but his effectiveness suffered. Seeing it happen in real time was no less panful, but he was able to start working through it.

Back to the list:

It's time to anticipate. Athletes do creative visualization before the actual event. You can do the same thing. Playing it out beforehand actually helps your nervous system get familiar with future events.

When my kids were young, we visited my parents and my wife's parents several times a year. They lived close to each other which was a blessing and a curse. Lots of family dynamics at play. Triggers ready and waiting.

We decided to anticipate everything that would piss us off. We wrote them down and numbered them. We decided to call out the number to each other whenever one of those things happened. Call it In-law Bingo.

The result ... those things happened and instead of getting angry, we laughed. It became a game instead of hurt feelings and ruined dinners. It didn't work perfectly, but it helped alot.

Run it through in your mind. They will say this ... and I will feel that. You may still take the bait ... but with practice, eventually you will avoid the hook.

If you actually take the time to do this exercise you will see a result. Before you walk into a room, take a few deep belly breaths, ground yourself in who you are (you are not your triggers) and walk into the room ready for whatever happens.

HE/SHE WHO STAYS GROUNDED AND CENTERED IN ANY GIVEN SITUATION ... WINS.

WHAT DO YOU NEED TO BE AT YOUR BEST?

After a few sessions with my clients, it's time to discuss what they need in order to be at their best. It is different for everyone. Of course, there are a few universal items on the list: exercise, downtime, connection ... but some things are more important than other so you.

"Tell me a time when you were at your best? What was working? What ingredients went into that version of you?" might be how I begin this conversation.

The following are examples from clients that work for them.

Client One: Yoga, Meditation, and Clean Food.

If he skipped a few days or ate like crap his A.D.D. was off the charts.

Client Two: Exercise and Sleep.

He noticed that when he partied with his friends during the week, he was nervous, short-fused and scattered at work. Later he discovered Mondays kind of sucked if Saturday night was out of hand.

Client Three: Heavy weights, MMA and a competitive sport.

He was chock full of energy and stress.

Client Four: Family Time and Running

Running gave her time alone to think and being with her family grounded her in something bigger than her job.

Me: I get up at 5:15 am. Meditation, Journaling, Reading, Exercise, coffee by my fish tank before I greet any people. Every day … non-negotiable. I joke that I don't wake up Mark J. Silverman, grounded and centered Executive Coach. I create him every day.

What is yours?

Commit to making time for yourself. You have to be on the list so you can be your best for everyone who counts on you.

"Yeah, like for me, I've got to take a walk. I've got to sleep at least eight, ideally, nine hours at night. I need a lot of sleep. And I need to have a meal with someone I love. If I do those three things, then no matter what's going on in my life, I can manage to mostly stay centered. It's interesting because the instinct is the opposite. When things are really going haywire, you tend to sleep exercise less. That's when you should double down on your recipe."

Kim Scott
Mastering Overwhelm Podcast, episode 25:
"The Art of Radical Candor"
https://bit.ly/3RqOO2T

For access to worksheets and other resources go to
https://bit.ly/46r8u8u

Chapter 10

DECIDE/CREATE YOURSELF

"I keep a little sticky note on my computer screen that asks, "Am I being the person I want to be right now?" Under that it says who that person is and I have these things listed. I want to be caring, I want to be empathetic, I want to be reasonable. I want to be a listener, I want to be fact based, I want to be balanced. I want to be a curious leader and learner and I want to throw sunshine, not a shadow. I have that in front of me, which helps me make sure that I keep on my track."

Garry Ridge
The Rising Leader Podcast episode 14:
"The Heart of a Servant-Leader"
https://bit.ly/3Gi89uf

As we discussed in the last chapter, your conditioned self, your ego is not who you truly are. Your personality is a series of experiences and choices that has you show up in a certain way. It is focused on your survival at all costs. It is also fungible. We get to change and grow.

EGO IS THE CAUSE OF ALL YOUR PROBLEMS.

You want to be right.

You want things to be fair.

You want credit.

You want to be respected.

You want control.

Your entire day, whether you realize it or not, is spent managing the outside world to fit how you think it should be (need it to be) for you to be happy, safe, loved or satisfied.

That's not just you, that is all of us.

If you get the world and its inhabitants to comply, how long does the happy, safe, loved or satisfied last?

The problem is, the world just won't cooperate.

"Pain is inevitable, suffering is optional," as the Buddhists say.

In other words, there is not alot we can do to avoid feeling sadness, anger, guilt, shame, frustration, or anxiety. They are part of our human experience. The truth is, if we mute those feelings we mute joy, love, peace and warmth.

The suffering comes when we fight against our natural emotions or fight against what is in the world. If you find yourself saying, "It shouldn't be this way," you are suffering. A more useful perspective is, "It is this way, it sucks, this is what I am going to do about it."

A true Zen Buddhist would go a step further and say, "It is this way, neither good or bad, This is how I will respond." But that is another book and much deeper practice.

On that note here are a few powerful places to start.

- *The Daily Stoic* - Ryan Holiday.

- *The Power of Now* - Eckhart Tolle.

- *Loving What Is* - Byron Katie.

- *Living Untethered* - Michal Singer.

- *Awareness* - Anthony deMello

All your "suffering" is because you want the outside world to be a certain way so you can feel a certain way inside. Unfortunately, it is ass backwards. It is an inside game.

"The three most powerful words in my life, and once I got comfortable with them, my life changed, are "I don't know." And when I got comfortable with those three words, "I don't know," I learned I need all the help I can get. How do I get people to help me? Well, if you serve them, they will help you. If I am dedicated to helping them, then I think they'll help me."

Garry Ridge
The Rising Leader Podcast episode 14:
"The Heart of a Servant-Leader"
https://bit.ly/3Gi89uf

"You can be right or you can be happy?"

~ **Gerald Jampolsky**

Translated for work: "Do you want to be right or do you want to be effective?"

Remember, the one who is grounded and centered (handles their triggers) holds the power in any situation.

I am not saying that we shouldn't strive to make our workplace fair, set boundaries, and garner respect, I am saying that we need to temper our demands so we are not fighting what should be and miss how we can impact what could be.

Getting triggered leaks power. While you are focused on how a thing "shouldn't be this way," your ability to affect change is diminished.

"Acceptance is the key to my serenity."

~ **AA**

"When you argue with reality, you only lose 100% of the time."

~ **Byron Katie**

Resistance to a thing wastes time, energy, and resources. Resistance to a problem, means you have two problems. This is the cause of your unhappiness.

Get this, and it will change your life.

Have I beat the subject to death yet? Truly get this point and *you will be happier.*

A few questions to ask yourself to drop the argument with what is and get back to effective quickly.

- Does it really affect me or does it just affect my ego?
- Whose problem is it really?
- If it does affect me, how does it really affect me?
- What can I really do about it?
- Do you *really* need to set a boundary or make an ask (good use of my political capital?)?
- Is it a good use of my political capital (hill I want to die on)?

MY (WORK) VERSION OF AA'S THE SERENITY PRAYER

G-D GRANT ME THE SERENITY TO ACCEPT THE THINGS I CANNOT CHANGE (REALITY),

THE COURAGE TO CHANGE THE THINGS I CAN (AND WANT TO)

AND THE WISDOM TO NOT TAKE THE BAIT.

"Early in my career everything was a nail and I was a hammer. I had to win, it had to be my way. That's where I started to realize that I was the problem. I was digging my heels in, or I wanted to be the smart one in the room I learned quickly, you have to focus on the outcome and try to remove all the friction to get there as quickly as possible. It that was a learning experience. Definitely after I got married, that that that helped in realizing that it's not about it's not about always being right. It's about getting the right outcome."

John Sapone
The Rising Leader Podcast episode 16:
"The Making of a Sales Leader"
https://bit.ly/47yVjE6

THE MAIN REASON WE FIGHT WITH WHAT'S "OUT THERE," IS BECAUSE WE ARE UNCOMFORTABLE WITH WHAT IS "IN HERE."

GROUNDED AND CENTERED WINS EVERY RACE

"It's kind of an intuition. But then it's also, there's a little bit of this concept of importance and urgency that I try and pay attention to. So, there's some things that seem important, but they're really just kind of an urgent thing that aren't that important.

The more that you can be present, and don't have all this frenetic energy and anxiety built up because you just feel like there's so many things going on the more that you can be making these quick, precise decisions in a calm manner, the more that you can decide which things are just urgent and can wait or they can be passed off and delegated versus the more important aspects of the business that need to be addressed."

Jefferson K. Rogers, CEO JKR Windows
The Rising Leader Podcast episode 11:
"Intuition, Health, and Leadership"
https://bit.ly/3sGMitj

Okay, Zen Master Flash, how do I get there?

Remember the human mind and how it's a drunk monkey stung by a scorpion? Being "in here" can be rough unless you learn to be with yourself.

It's time to create what I call, a homing device.

I want you to develop a tool to get our of the monkey mind (your reactions) and back to reality in any given situation. The books I've mentioned here in the text will offer a deeper dive. *It would be the greatest investment in the quality of your life you will ever make if you do explore it further.*

I was working with a client who had done an amazing job of moving through emotional reactions in conversations with the CEO and in leadership teams. Now it was time for some refinement. He had mentioned that he wants to work on *"being more present."*

Mark: *"You can't be more present. You can either be present or not."*

Client rolling his eyes: *"I knew you were going to say that the minute that left my mouth."*

Mark: *"How do you know you are present?"*

Client: *"I'm not on my phone or doing email in a meeting."*

Mark: *"Yes and ... check your breathing. If you are breathing from your chest, you aren't present, if you are breathing from your belly ... more likely present. Check your posture. Wiggle your toes and fingers. Look at your surroundings or the people in the room (or on screen). Stay there. When you forget, come back. Just like meditation."*

Client: *"Okay, I get it."*

That's it, wiggle your toes, touch your fingers together, breathe deeply from your belly, feel your feelings, and you are present. You may still not be comfortable, just notice that.

> ## HINT: MOST OF US ARE TOO UNCOMFORTABLE TO BE PRESENT, THAT'S WHY IT TAKES PRACTICE.

SO HOW DO WE GET GOOD AT THIS?

Practice!

"Mark, how are you so grounded and centered all the time?"

I actually wake up like Eeyore. I love my life and what I do but I am not a naturally happy or positive person. I must create this version of Mark every day if I want to live the life I say I want. I have to do the work to be the person my clients need me to be.

I get up at 5:15am, grab a cup of coffee and head to my meditation cushion. I read something worthwhile, journal for 20 minutes then I meditate. After that I exercise and have a healthy breakfast.

My morning routine is non-negotiable because I love the impact it has on my life.

- How do you want to show up?
- What effect do you want to have on people?
- What do you want to create?

If you want to be an Instagram model you will need to exercise like a fiend, eat like a rabbit, wax in places I don't even want to think about, and have very, very, good lighting. You will have to be willing to take 1000s of photos of yourself to get the right one. You will have to study algorithms and trends and dedicate yourself to them for a few years.

Doesn't seem so attractive anymore, does it?

Steve Chandler says, "You don't admire someone's muscles, you admire their dedication to the gym."

So, let me ask you. Who do you admire? I mean, *really* admire for all the *right* reasons?

One of the people I admire is Brett Culp, who I mentioned in a story earlier in the book. He is a professional keynote speaker and filmmaker. I noticed his videos on social media and started following him. I loved his confident manner on stage, but more than that, I loved how kind he was. I loved his mission to make every person in that audience feel seen, acknowledged, and lifted.

I wanted to have that impact on people.

When he guested on my podcast, I introduced him as my "Spirit Animal."

We have since become good friends and learn from each other.

Another "Spirit Animal," for me is Rabbi Menachem Mendel Schneerson, the Lubavitcher Rebbe. He was the leader of the sect of Judaism we raised our children in. He was in his nineties and every Sunday stood for hours and gave out dollar bills as blessings to the 1000s of people wanting to be in his presence. People held onto those precious spiritual symbols for decades. One day he was asked, "Rebbe, don't you get tired standing out here for hours in the cold greeting so many people?"

His response, "Who gets tired counting diamonds?"

I thought … who does a man have to be to see endless lines of needy New Yorkers as diamonds? The beauty of it reduced me to tears.

Knowing who I admire … you can see what I value.

My reading, the people I surround myself, and my practices are in line with helping me be more like the people I admire.

❝ Practice, practice, practice. Practicing taking action, even when you are not feeling it, will strengthen your ability to not be influenced by your temporary emotional state. Feeling good is not a requirement, it is a result. This is practice. My practice is to create the space necessary so I have the inner resources to give 100 percent."

~ **Tony Bonnici,** *The Dojo*

WHO IS YOUR ALTER EGO OR AVATAR

When I watched Brett or the Rebbe, I didn't say, "I wish I could be as kind and impactful as them." I got introspective. "Who do I need to be to have that impact? What practices do I need to have in my life to show up that way? How do I need to see people to treat them in that way?"

And then I went about creating myself that way. I am a work in progress.

Todd Herman wrote a great book called, *The Alter Ego Effect – The Power of Secret Identities.* In the book he explains how so many great people in sports and history have modeled themselves after their heroes. They even carried talismans and reminders so they could bring that energy into every situation.

Let's Reflect

Who do you admire? Who moves you? Who are you jealous of?

Take some time and consider who they are and what it is about them that inspires you? Consider what they have to do, what they are willing to give up, and what support they get to be who they are.

Then consider... are you willing? In order to be more like The Rebbe or Brett, I must let go of my habit of judging harshly. A work in progress.

Now let's go about creating the practices and routines that will create you to be the best version of yourself.

Remember, as a leader, you need to be who your team, your family, or the situation need you to be.

It's not easy. Steve Chandler again,
"The answer to how = yes."

Commit first, you will figure it out as you go. That's all any of us can do.

In any given situation, ask better questions:

- Do you need to be curious in a conversation?
- Do you need to be courageous in action?
- Do you need to be understanding to connect?
- Do you need to be decisive to lead?

Your brain will wonder ... "How am I going to do this?" Don't take the bait. Replace it with "Who do I need to be?" "How do I need to show up?"

Watch magic happen.

YOU AT YOUR BEST

I shared what I need to do to be at my best every day. What is it for you?

- Is it a morning practice?
- Is it exercise?
- Is it food?
- Family time?
- Is it contemplation?

- Is it connection?

- Is it creativity?

- What lights you up?

- What gets you grounded?

Start small.

If it is meditation and it's new for you, how about one minute a day for seven days?

If it's food and your diet is terrible, can you just give up soda?

Commitment and consistency are key. If you say you are going to do it, do it. If you bite off more than you are willing to chew, pare it back to what you are willing to do.

Remember, you don't have to do anything alone, get a buddy or an accountability partner.

VALUES

"Live by your values and everything else will fall into place."

~ Unknown

My friend Tony Bonnici, author of *The Dojo: The Ancient Wisdom of Integrative Leadership for the Modern Entrepreneur"* divides his reader's focus into four quadrants or values: Work/Legacy, Physical, Relationship and Spiritual. He does this to make sure that his clients are successful in all areas of their lives.

We need to make decisions and choices every day. The best way I have found to make those decisions easier is to know what is important.

When we got divorced, my ex-wife and I created an unshakable commitment to our children. They come first in every situation. All of my choices, from where I lived to who I dated to work travel I accepted, were grounded in that value.

That commitment changed our relationship. We were able to make decisions, disagree and come to agreement, and let go of petty hurts faster.

What do you value?

Family?

Spirituality?

Health?

Integrity?

If you didn't get clear in Know Yourself, do that now.

Write your values down. Live by them.

A clear set of values makes it easier to set boundaries, resolve conflict and navigate life.

LEADING YOU: LEAD YOURSELF

VICTIM OR OWNER

One of the most important distinctions in all of coaching is the difference between Reactive or Victim mindset versus a Creative or Owner mentality. Steve Chandler, coach and author explores this in his teachings with directness and humor. I give out cases of his books and now he has released *The Very Best of Steve Chandler*, so you can get all the wisdom in one place. I highly recommend it.

When we talk about "leading yourself" we are referring to the shift from reacting to what life throws at you to taking an active role in creating the circumstance you want. That includes your inner talk as well.

Let's look at some of the hallmarks of each so we can recognize where we fall into the trap before I have you confront your to-do list.

Victem Mindset

Dislike Change

"Fixed" Mindset

Pessimistic

Complain

Blame Others

Life Happens TO Them

Defined By Their Past

"Poor Me" - Expects Sympathy

Owner Mindset

Embrace Change

"Growth" Mindset

Optimistic

Look For Opportunities

Take Full Responsibility (For Their Happiness)

Problems Are Challenges/Opportunities

Present And Future Focused

In Touch With Reality

Victem Behavior

Focuses On "The Story" -
Not The Facts

History Focused

Externalizes Blame

Blames Others

Makes Excuses

Waits & Hopes

Ignores/Compartmentalizes/
Numbs Out

Owner Behavior

Acknowledges Facts -
"Powerfully In Touch With Reality"

Learns Lessons

Takes Responsibility

Solutions Orientated

Future Focused

Victem Language

"Life is unfair. That's just life."

"I'm trying to *get through*
the week."

I'm swamped. I'm stressed,
I'm overwhelmed."

"Should" "Ought" "Obligated"

Uses the word THEY

Owner Language

"I *get* to pick up my kids from school."

"I *choose* to go to work."

"I *want* to work on this relationship with
my spouse/son/etc..."

"I made a decision to commit to _____."

"If there is a problem,
how will I create a solution?"

Uses the word WE

The challenge is recognizing where you fall into the trap of reactive thinking and consciously choosing a different way of responding.

It is a choice, once you see it. Sometimes it is juicer to play the victim for a bit. If you want something different than you have always had… time to get that creator online.

This will be important when we "take ownership" of our to-do list in the next section.

ONLY 10s

Welcome to the Only 10s portion of our program.

I've been teaching this methodology since my "Ah-ha!" moment in 2015 where I discovered that I am 100% responsible for my life. *Only 10s* the book has since sold over 75,000 copies and you can get yours free on the Resources page.

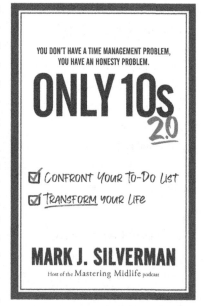

We will be using this methodology to triage your workload, clear overwhelm and help you focus on the things that are important. That includes your health, well-being, family and spirit.

A few things I'd like you to keep in mind as we begin to live a "created life":

- I create my own overwhelm and my own freedom.

- I only do what I want to do and don't do what I don't want to do, only always.

- The thing is never the thing. I only always want to get a reward (outcome) or avoid a consequence.

- My life and circumstances are my responsibility. Not "fault," but responsibility. I may not have dealt the hand, but it is my job to play that hand as best I can.

- By acknowledging the part I played in creating a situation, I take back the power to influence the situation.

"Drop by drop the pot is filled, likewise the wise person, gathering it little by little, fills themselves with good."

~ Buddha

Drop by drop, you got yourself here, the good news is that drop by drop you can get yourself out.

- Overweight? How did you treat your health over the last several years?

- Boss doesn't respect your work? How have you shown up to influence that outcome?

- Constantly working long hours to clean up your team's work? How good was your coaching, teaching and leading in recent past?

THIS SECTION IS A SUMMARY OF THE ONLY 10S PROCESS.

> You can download a free copy of the book here:
> https://bit.ly/46r8u8u
>
> And you can watch video resources
> from the book here:
> https://bit.ly/46r8u8u

Your problem isn't too much to do and too many people pulling on your time, it's that you are not honest about what you want to do, are willing to do, or should be doing. Your problem is that you don't set boundaries, take on too much, fail to delegate, and overwork yourself out of some fear or should.

"Busy-ness = Laziness"

~ Steve Chandler

Your problem is you do not take the time to plan and prioritize, and stick to that plan.

Your problem is that you live a "default life" rather than a "created life."

I know that was harsh ... bordering on scolding. You are a high-achiever, you create, you get stuff done, and you are basically an honest person. I didn't mean to insult you.

I meant to get your attention ... because few of us really take the time and energy to fully, consciously create the life we want.

YOU DON'T HAVE A TIME MANAGEMENT PROBLEM, YOU HAVE AN HONESTY PROBLEM.

Now that we are friends again, let's up the commitment level a notch or two.

MINI ONLY 10s COURSE

- List out everything on your to do list for the next one week (work and personal).
- Weight each item from 1 to 10 in order of priority and importance.
- Throw out everything on your list that's numbered from 1 to 9.
- Repeat this at the start of each day to prioritize what to focus on each day.

For this exercise, please use my definition of a 10.

A 10 needs to be done.

A 10 needs to be done by me

A 10 needs to be done by me TODAY

Or

I really want to do it.

Be ruthless in naming your 10s.

Remember, everything we do is to get a reward or avoid a consequence.

Everything.

When you get this, you will start to see why things are on your plate, and the secret to why they shouldn't be.

FALSE 10s

- Also known as qualifiers or distractions.
- I really 'should' do this.
- It's a great idea BUT I really don't want to do this (9.9s).
- Other people's priorities.
- Busy work.
- Placeholders.

Look for the thing behind the thing. Falling for the qualifiers will drive you to overwhelm.

Really look out for 9s. They seem important, but somehow, never get done. They just suck your attention and make you feel bad about not doing them. Get rid of them.

Guard your to-do list like a junk yard dog. Interrogate your items like a criminal.

What's on your list because:

- You couldn't set a boundary?
- You want to be liked or seen as productive?
- You were afraid to delegate?
- You are lying to yourself about actually doing it?

If you look at all the work we have done throughout this book, you will start to see why some of those things are on your list. Confronting your to-do list takes courage, willingness to disappoint other people, difficult conversations and making choices.

The result is freedom to focus on what is important to you.

What is not on your list, that should be?

FIVE LEVERS FOR SUSTAINABLE SUCCESS

1. Your Energy Levels – Health and vitality

2. Your Focus – The ability to concentrate your energy on the right things

3. Your Efficiency – Traction. Creativity. Effectiveness.

4. Your Courage – Going beyond your conditioned limits

5. Your Support System – Your foundation

If you want to be at your best, you need to prioritize the things that get you there. If any of these areas are lacking, you are spinning your wheels.

"Half the distance takes you twice as long"

~ Eagles from "After the Thrill is Gone"

Take a moment and rate each of the five levers you have to create success as red, yellow or green. If it's green, awesome. Reflect on how that supports your life and productivity. If it's red, how is it holding you back?

None of this matters. Not the success, accolades, or money, if your life isn't full of joy and fulfillment. Miserable success is not success.

So, let's get you to and keep you at the top of your game. In order to get the most out of the five levers you need to put *you* first. It is being selfish in the right ways.

HOW TO FILL YOUR TANK

"Burnout is 100% preventable. Most of us are driven in our aspirations out of fear of what will not happen if we don't get to the finish line. We have this mythology that comes from the human survival perspective that if we don't put enough time and energy into this, then we don't deserve to win, which is a complete lie.

You got about 20 or 30 years of functional reserve on board physically and psychologically before you blow yourself up. Another trick that the body plays on us is that the nervous system makes us feel that the absence of having suffered or blown ourselves up yet, means that everything's okay. It not, because we're losing capacity over time, but we don't know it. The nervous system only reveals to us something of sufficient magnitude to let us know what's there. You could be running on fumes and not even know it and get up the next day with adrenal burnout, which is automatically your 12 months out of the game recovering. We really need a proactive view of the cumulative impact of stress and strain over time, and not buy into the mythology of the survival mind which is that you're gonna blow, that it's only a matter of time, and the time where you need to investigate what the hidden time bomb is when he got the time to do it. Otherwise, it's going to be a forced sabbatical.

The biggest boogeyman in all of this is that we think we're gonna lose something if we slow down because everybody else is running faster. Nothing could be farther from the truth. We need to learn to develop confidence and certainty in ourselves, we need to know that we're not at the end of the puppet master pulling our strings. It's what I call the Hustler's Hoax, where we feel that more, faster, quicker gets us to the finish line with greater ease. It's complete fabrication, because the reality is, if you pace yourself over time, and you're developing your skills to a capacity where you learn how to win the game, then you still got a huge runway in front of you to amass a lifetime of experiences that few people will ever experience in their entire life. To do that, you have to be able to identify the mythology of what most "experts" say. That may seem correct, but unfortunately, it has never delivered on its promise. It's an absolute fabrication. You're actually supporting someone, perhaps even one step before they make the breakthrough to blow themselves up in one of three ways. Number one, they have a catastrophic relationship failure, because they didn't nurture the relationship along the way. Two, everybody's heard a story of someone having a catastrophic health event. People are having heart attacks and strokes in their late 30s and early 40s. That's all preventable. Just when you're getting your momentum then you blow yourself up with financial ruin. You go all in on something, you risk everything and you ultimately suffer the fate. That's 100% garbage."

Dr. Jeff Spencer
The Rising Leader Podcast episode 37:
"Playing the Bigger Game"
https://bit.ly/3QVeCQL

1. Relationships

- Make time for your friends and family
- Hold sacred your relationship with your significant other
- Be there for your children

2. Health

- What are you putting in your body?
- How are you moving your body, every day?

3. Groundedness and Centeredness

- What daily consciousness exercise and practices are you committed to?

4. Spirit

- It does not need to be G-d or Religion. How do you connect with a greater perspective than your human mind?

5. Creativity

- What do you do to nurture your soul every day? Is it art, music, cooking? Creativity in one place translates to all others.

Reflection

What is one thing you could drop out that would make a difference in one of the above areas? What one thing can you add to fill your tank. Small steps create amazing results. The trick is to take that one step.

Your job is to balance the needs of your significant other, your children, your friends, your family and, most importantly, yourself with the needs of your job, your team, your peers, your boss, and the organization.

Lead with your values as your compass. Let them guide your choices. You will be the leader the people in your life need you to be and thrive in your role.

For access to worksheets and other resources go to
https://bit.ly/46r8u8u

CONCLUSION

> MUCH OF "LEADERSHIP" IS
> JUST A SERIES OF DIFFICULT CONVERSATIONS.
> IF YOU ARE NOT SUCCESSFUL (YET) AS A LEADER,
> YOU ARE NOT HAVING ENOUGH OF THEM.

I think you may have noticed early on in this book is that we focused on communication. In most of the challenging situations we played out, an honest, possibly tough, conversation is the solution.

Giving feedback (over and over), speaking your mind, cleaning up a mess, asking for help, getting clarification, setting a boundary, making an agreement ... all just saying what needs to be said. Finding the courage to be honest in your relationships, will build those relationships.

Speaking up has another side effect. It set's you free.

I felt like a prisoner and a victim of circumstance most of my life. I had no idea it was because I twisted myself into a pretzel to be what I thought the world wanted me to be. Figuring out who I was, what I valued and how I wanted to spend the precious minutes of my life was the first step to freedom. Learning to have the requisite conversations to actually live those values and desires was step two.

Step three involved healing and inner work so as not to be trapped in the conditioning of the past. We did a little of that here in this book in the sections on contemplation and reflection.

I want you to be free. That's my mission in life, for you to know that you are ok as you are, and that you are loved and free. It goes on the back of my gravestone.

The irony is "Leadership Skills," will set you free. Taking action, speaking up, connecting with people, learning about yourself and creating your life and work accordingly will lead to your freedom and fulfillment.

What the hell good is all the success if you're not enjoying it … at least most of the time?

1% BETTER EVERY DAY

Remember, we started this conversation with leadership being a "learned skill." Step by step, be kind to yourself, be willing to make mistakes and acknowledge yourself for stepping up. Few do. Just be a little better than you were yesterday... the compound effect will amaze you.

I'll leave you with this conversation from *The Rising Leader Podcast* with Healthcare Executive Geoffrey Roche:

Mark: I don't like the cliche conversations we have about leadership. There are these labels put on leadership that make it daunting for people that make a nurse say 'I'm not a leader, because I don't have these traits or these titles, or these badges of honor or this attitude.

Geoffrey: When I think about my leadership, and when I think about the leaders that I have most been attracted to, what has always been clear for them, and for me, is purpose and meaning. When you really understand your purpose, and your meaning, as a leader, you realize that it is all about the people. And that whether you have a title or not, you have purpose, and you have meaning to impact everything around you. And you also have a purpose, to fulfill whatever your dreams are, and at the same time, help others fulfill theirs.

This may be controversial. When I look at a lot of the major authors of leadership they make it seem like it's so hard to get there. And that bothers me so much. Because I see it in our society so often, where people will say, 'I can't reach that, I've read this, and it makes it seem like I can't do that." The reality of it is that if we embed mentorship, if we embrace coaching, if we embed support to one another into all facets of an organization, anybody can reach it. And so, I truly think that we have taught and spoken about leadership in many of the wrong ways for so long. And it's people like you, and it's people like Meredith Bell and others who actually have understood this from the very start, that it's truly about the heart. And it's truly about connection. And when you establish that meaningful connection, you can lead like no other."

Geoffrey Roche
The Rising Leader Podcast episode 49:
"Heart-Centered Leadership"
https://bit.ly/3tNPHXF

You have what it takes to lead like no other!

LET'S CONNECT FURTHER

Again, we touched on quite a lot in our time together. There is a deeper dive on every topic. We can do a whole course on giving feedback or delegation. You can spend decades deepening your meditation practice and your connection to something greater.

I have created a Resource Page where you can find more books for those deeper dives. You will also find the worksheets and supporting videos. There will be links to *The Rising Leader,* *Mastering Overwhelm,* and *Mastering Midlife* podcasts where I speak with experts on everything from sex to money management.

You will also find information on **The Rising Leader Course,** great for your team to create shared practices and language. There is even a place for you to sign up to have a conversation with me about working together.

YOU CAN REACH ME WITH QUESTIONS AT SUPPORT@MARKJSILVERMAN.COM

My hope is that you use this as a jumping off point. No matter how seasoned or inexperienced you are, we are all beginners starting from where we are.

That's it.

I love you. I appreciate you. You are amazing ... go live that way.

Mark

MARK'S RECOMMENDED READING LIST

Abrahams, Matt. *Think Fast, Talk Smarter*

Alfero, Teo. *The Wolf Connection*

Appleby, Helen. *The Unwritten Rules of Women's Leadership*

Bonnici, Tony. *The Dojo: The Ancient Wisdom of Integrative Leadership for the Modern Entrepreneur*

Bungay Stanier, Michael. *The Coaching Habit* and *How to Work With Almost Anyone*

Chandler, Steve. *The Best of Steve Chandler, Time Warrior,* and *Reinventing Yourself*

Cohn, Alisa. *From Start Up to Grown Up.*

Crowley, Mark C. *Leading From the Heart*

DeMello, Anthony. *Awareness*

Holiday, Ryan. *The Daily Stoic*

Katie, Byron. *Loving What Is*

Lencioni, Patrick. *The Five Dysfunctions of a Team,* and *The Six Types of Working Genius*

Litvin, Rich and Steve Chandler. *The Prosperous Coach*

Scott, Kim. *Radical Candor*

Singer, Michael. *The Untethered Soul,* and *Living Untethered*

Tolle, Eckhart. *The Power of Now*

Wickman, Gino and Mark C. *Winters, Rocket Fuel*

ACKNOWLEDGMENTS

I learned leadership in the fast-paced high-tech environment of the past few decades.

I also learned leadership attending numerous classes, workshops, and retreats. I have read hundreds of books on the topic. I have done decades of my own inner work and skill-building.

And I have learned the most, in real life situations with some of the most incredible front-line managers and senior executives to ever take on the mantle of "leader."

Tom Mendoza, Dan Warmenhoven, Greg Collins, Michael O'Donnell, Beth Perlman, Dennis Sheehan, Frank Slootman, Dave Schneider, Kevin Haverty, John Sapone, Denise Cox, Eric Mann, Kurt Greening, Rob Salmon, Helen Appleby, Roderick Jefferson, Phil Adair, Brian Spitzer, Nancy Gretzinger and Stan Bromely...to name a few.

I also believe, no leader can do it on their own. You must have a posse who keep you grounded, love you unconditionally, and help you grow beyond what you thought possible.

Tony Bonnici, Christina Berkley, Helen Appleby, Katie Nelson, Jen Dalton, and Brandon T. Adams ... thank you for being in my corner.

Seema Bharwani for turning our conversations into the clarity that became this book's structure.

Patti M. Hall, Miracle Worker

ABOUT MARK J. SILVERMAN

Mark anchors his brand at www.markjsilverman.com. He is widely accepted as a stellar podcast host and interviewer. The three iterations of his podcast and the extensive guest list are a feature of this, Mark's second book.

Mastering Midlife Podcast

Mastering Overwhelm Podcast

The Rising Leader Podcast

Mark's first book ***Only 10s*** (and ***Only 10s 2.0***) have sold more than 75,000 copies and are the foundation for his Mastering Overwhelm talk and workshops.

Mark J. Silverman came to executive coaching and speaking after a successful career in technology where he generated over $90,000,000 for fast growing start-ups by bringing together executives, technical leaders and stakeholders to close complex multimillion dollar sales.

As an Executive Coach for over 10 years, enjoying a full roster of clients, Mark is committed to helping CEOs, Senior Leadership and Fast-rising High Achievers leverage their resources and team for greater impact while creating sustainable success in all areas with their lives.

Made in United States
Orlando, FL
06 March 2024

44454656R00115